AMONG FRIENDS

You can help make your church a warmer place.

INCLUDES QUESTIONS FOR GROUP DISCUSSION

NAVPRESS

A MINISTRY OF THE NAVIGATORS
P.O. BOX 6000, COLORADO SPRINGS, COLORADO 80934

The Navigators is an international Christian organization. Jesus Christ gave His followers the Great Commission to go and make disciples (Matthew 28:19). The aim of The Navigators is to help fulfill that commission by multiplying laborers for Christ in every nation.

NavPress is the publishing ministry of The Navigators. NavPress publications are tools to help Christians grow. Although publications alone cannot make disciples or change lives, they can help believers learn biblical discipleship, and apply what they learn to their lives and ministries.

Cover illustration: Doug Bowles

Printed in the United States of America

FOR A FREE CATALOG OF
NAVPRESS BOOKS & BIBLE STUDIES,
CALL TOLL FREE 800-366-7788 (USA)
or 800-263-2664 (CANADA)

Contents

Authors

James Hinkle has served on the Bible faculty of York College since 1979, ministering on weekends to the Davenport Church of Christ. He holds a master's degree in New Testament Greek from Harding Graduate School of Religion in Memphis, Tennessee, and the doctorate of ministry from Fuller Theological Seminary in Pasadena, California. James and his wife, Harriet, have three children and live in York, Nebraska.

Tim Woodroof holds a master's degree in clinical psychology from Texas A & M University and a Ph.D. in community and human relations from the University of Nebraska. Since 1983, he has ministered to the Lincoln Church of Christ in Lincoln, Nebraska. Tim and his wife, Julie, have three children.

In 1980, James and Tim began Living in Harmony Ministries—an effort designed to promote stronger relationships in local congregations. Through seminars, a video series, and written materials, this ministry has benefitted hundreds of congregations throughout the country. *Among Friends* is an outgrowth of that work and the result of many years of thought and ministry in the area of Christian relationships.

Acknowledgments

We would like to thank the following people for their help with *Among Friends*: Angie Gray, Anne Gray, and Janine Michael for typing and transcribing; Lagard Smith for his encouragement and advice; Jim Woodroof and Bob Lawrence for their reading of the manuscript; Bruce Nygren and his staff at NavPress for their kindness and persistence in refining this manuscript; and a special word of thanks to our wives for more than we can say and more than they can know.

Preface

In the age of the drive-in church and televangelism, the idea of a caring community of believers has become almost quaint. Many people today see faith as an essentially private matter, requiring only a relationship with God. Some may say, "I have a very personal religion. My faith is my own business." Such people see involvement with other Christians as optional. Fellowship is no longer a necessary part of contemporary Christian living. Faith has become so privatized that for many "church" is something as easily done alone in front of the TV as in the company of other Christians.

The Church of the first century was cut from different cloth. It was a relationship place. It was a family of believers. It was a shelter to which Christians turned when they wanted to be among friends. They called each other "brother" and "sister." Acceptance and healing were found in their midst. Confession and hospitality were commonly practiced.

If this is not descriptive of the Church today, it should be. The fact that some Christians feel uncomfortable with the intimate community portrayed in the New Testament indicates a misunderstanding of what the Church is all about. The Church is more than its creeds and ceremonies and sanctuaries. It is *people* who are learning to love each other as their Lord has loved them. True religion is not just private and vertical, it is communal and horizontal as well.

A vibrant Christian fellowship is not only the expectation of the gospel but its validation as well. Our most powerful answer to the skeptic's doubt is not found in reasoned arguments but in real relationships. When the Church is a gathering of true friends, it offers the world its most compelling apologetic.

It is to encourage such vibrant fellowship that this book is written. May God use this work to His glory and to the benefit of His Church.

Discussion, Reflection, and Action

At the end of each chapter you will find questions for personal study and group discussion. We hope they will help you get involved personally and actively with the material in this book. We've tried to write flexible questions that can be used with all kinds of groups—from those that are just starting out to those that have been meeting for some time and have developed good discussion skills. Since you know your group best, it's up to you to decide how to shape the discussion. If your group is one that delves deeply into a question and wrestles with it until you know what you think and what you are going to do about it, select just a few of the questions for each chapter. If the group members find they have less to say about each question, take advantage of the many questions available.

Treat the questions as discussion starters, not as the only ones that can be asked about the chapter. Group leaders should always be thinking of questions that help their groups reflect on their own needs.

We have divided the questions into three categories:

"Chapter Discussion" includes questions intended to help the group personally apply the material in the chapter. We believe that if group members support each other, they will be able to apply the principles in this book and make them work in their local church. Groups that plan to cover only a few questions deeply should stick to this section for the most part.

The questions in "Personal Bible Search" are intended to be done during your private devotional time or family Bible study. These questions can serve as a foundation for the group discussion. If you study them beforehand, they will help make your discussion more biblically oriented. If you have time or if you find some of these questions especially helpful, you can include them in your discussion.

"Personal Reflection and Action" includes questions that encourage you to think further about the subject of the chapter. The section also offers ways of putting the material into practice. Individuals or the whole group can use this material.

CHAPTER ONE

The Church in Crisis

A few years ago, Dr. Francis Schaeffer made this shocking statement:

> Unless the Church changes its form and gets back to community and the sharing of lives personally, the Church is done.[1]

Why would an author of numerous books defending the Church issue such a dire warning about her future? Certainly, the Church has never lacked doomsayers. But when the stones are thrown by her most able defenders, it makes you wonder.

Was Dr. Schaeffer unaware of trends that seem to indicate the Church is alive and well? Megachurches are growing in our cities with congregations numbering in the thousands, supporting huge staffs and impressive ministries. Powerful media ministries, in spite of undeniable abuses, are reaching new audiences with the gospel of Jesus Christ. And after a hundred years of liberal theology, the Bible has withstood all attacks and is being granted—even in scholarly circles—the respect and trust it deserves. Do these current trents sound like the dying gasps of a Church that is almost "done"?

Unfortunately, many of us who love the Church cannot shrug off a growing conviction that Dr. Schaeffer is right. In spite of some wonderful things happening on the surface of Christ's Body, a sickness is spreading deep within her bones.

Case #1—Harry and Margaret are faithful members of the "Straight and Narrow Church" (not its real name, by the way). The group is theologically conservative, Bible-based, and truly interested in doing God's will. That interest has caused the church to focus primarily on matters of doctrine. Their highest goal is to worship right, and teach right, and live right.

Though the congregation is fervently evangelistic, it has not grown in size for a number of years. Twice in the past decade the church has split, each time over differences in what constitutes sound teaching. Each parting has left members wounded and angry. Though Harry and Margaret are committed to the church, they are uncomfortable with the way people have been treated. In Bible class, Harry has decided it is safer to keep quiet than to speak up and risk his brothers' and sisters' disapproval. Margaret is sometimes embarrassed to admit where she goes to church.

Case #2—John and Dorothy recently moved to town and have been attending the "Business as Usual Church" just down the road. The building is old and large (as are many of the members), the sermons traditional, and the music program good. Though John and Dorothy are members of this denomination, they have decided to shop for another church. In the months they have worshiped with this group, they have had little contact with members at worship services and none whatsoever outside the building. They want a group where they can meet people and develop friendships. Next week they will worship elsewhere, listening less to the sermon or the choir than to the degree of warmth and welcome extended by those who sit around them.

Case #3—George has been a member of the "I'm O.K./You're O.K. Church" for several years. Although the church's theology is a bit liberal for his tastes, other aspects of the group are much to his liking. He enjoys the informal atmosphere of the congregation and looks forward to the time in every service when the people exchange hugs and words of welcome. The minister is warm and charismatic and often talks about the importance of communicating acceptance and love.

Recently, however, George has questioned the sincerity of the church's fellowship. A severe bout of hepatitis confined him to the hospital and then to home. His recovery was slow and as a result he lost his job. During the most difficult weeks of his life, he heard nothing from the church. No visits, no calls, no cards. As far as he knew, no one had even missed him. When he finally called the church secretary to explain his circumstances, the church sent a check from its benevolence fund, although the postman rather than a brother made the delivery.

These are not isolated cases, but real situations found in every church. Liberal or conservative, large or small, rural or urban—you can change the setting but you won't change the problem. Ignore for a moment the congregations and focus on the people we have described. You know them. You've sat next to them and shared a song book. You've asked, "Whatever happened to _____?" six months after they fell through the cracks. You may have been one of these people at some point in your life.

Add up all the people in our churches who never find fellowship with those who long for a deeper fellowship, throw in those who watch conflict and dissension threatening what fellowship they do have—and you will understand why Dr. Schaeffer could write, "Unless the Church changes its forms and gets back to community and the sharing of lives personally, the Church is done."

He is exactly right. The greatest danger facing the Church today is neither doctrinal nor moral. It is relational. Not that doctrine is unimportant—we cannot build sound fellowship on unsound teaching. But there is more to Church life than the content of our beliefs. There is also the matter of how we relate to one another. It is possible to possess the gift of knowledge yet lack the gift of love. When that happens, we truly have nothing.

This is the crisis facing the Church today, the issue threatening not just our growth but our existence. We've lost our sense of family. We avoid sharing lives personally. We no longer see ourselves as a *community* of believers. The independence and isolation that afflicts our society has now infected the Kingdom of God. As a result, we find ourselves less and less comfortable with the Christ who calls us to love one another as He has loved us.

But if that is the reality of the Church today, it is not her ideal. A desire is growing to rediscover the meaning of fellowship and to reestablish a sense of community. Every night of the week in cities and towns throughout the country, small groups of Christians meet in homes to learn more about the Bible *and* each other. Christians are taking the "one another" passages seriously, attempting to recreate a New Testament fellowship. Preachers are calling their congregations to love not "with words or tongue but with actions and in truth" (1 John 3:18). Believers everywhere are ready to make the Church the relationship place God designed it to be.

Much of the motivation behind this renaissance of concern for a deeper fellowship in the Christian community is born of simple desperation. As relationships disintegrate in every other sphere of our society, Christ's followers are increasingly convinced they must offer a clear alternative. Divorce, domestic violence, teen suicides, and child abuse face today's fractured families. Stories of prejudice, warfare, and international tensions fill the newspapers and airwaves. Television and the movie industry seem obsessed with casual morals, compromised integrity, and uncontrolled brutality. We live in a dehumanizing, self-absorbed, and alienated world.

It seems at times that the Body of Christ lags not far behind. Christians drag one another to court, Church leaders slander each other on national television, congregations fight publicly. In nearly every church are people who have refused to speak to each other for years. Rather than being known for the quality of our relationships, we are famous for the quantity of our conflicts.

If Christians cannot provide vivid and compelling alternatives to decaying relationships in the world, the Church and the world are in serious trouble. Where else can the world turn to find a better way of relating to people, if not to the family of God? Where else will it hear a message about integrity, commitment, and love even of enemies, if not from the disciples of Jesus? It doesn't take a prophet to suggest that unless the Church influences relationships in the world, the world will influence relationships in the Church.

The time has come for the Church to find herself once again. Somewhere along the way we have taken a wrong turn. In the press to clarify dogma and enforce ethic and argue theology, we have overlooked something fundamental about ourselves. We are family, community, fellowship. Until we discover how to love each other, none of the rest really matters.

SECOND THINGS FIRST

On the Wednesday before Jesus was crucified, a Pharisee asked Him, "What is the most important thing in the world?" Immediately, Jesus answered, "'Love the Lord your God with all your heart and with all your soul and with all your mind.' This is the first and greatest commandment" (Matthew 22:37).

If religious commitment were just a matter of loving God, there would be far more religious people in the world today. To our great distress, however, Jesus did not limit the practice of religion to the way we feel about God. He gave a second command to go with the first, one that was equally great in His mind.

"And the second is like it: 'Love your neighbor as yourself'" (Matthew 22:39). The Pharisee asked for the *greatest* commandment. Evidently, Jesus felt He could not do justice to the question by responding with one and only one command. Certainly, love for God was primary in Christ's mind, but this second command was closely allied, complementing and completing the first. It is upon these *two* commandments that "all the Law and the Prophets hang" (verse 40). Jesus called it the "second command"—but second only in sequence, not in significance. In this matter, second things are also of first importance.

Like many of us, some of the Pharisees defined religion solely in terms of their relationship with God. Faith was a vertical business conducted between Heaven and earth. Not even a bleeding brother at the side of the road kept them from proper religious observance. Love of God was first, everything else a distant last.

The radical implication of Jesus' teaching is that authentic Christianity, unequivocal in its command to love God, is equally a matter of how we relate to each other. The tone of voice we use with one another, the respect we show, the forgiveness and tolerance we extend—these are the stuff of real religion as much as prayer and worship and theology. Religious life has a horizontal aspect. According to Jesus, it takes obedience on both fronts to walk rightly before God. We must exercise both a love for God and a love for people to avoid a crippled religion.

Yet even when Christians recognize the importance of loving others, we find the second command more difficult to keep than the first. The things which make us love God we won't always find in each other. God is loving. People often are not. We cannot depend (as we do with God) on their warmth toward us to kindle a reciprocal feeling in our own hearts. While God's nature makes Him eminently lovable, all of us know people who provoke just the opposite reaction. If we must wait for someone to turn lovable before obeying this command, we'll wait a long time for some folks. Though the command to love each other is just as important as the command to love God, it does seem more difficult.

The difficulty of the task, however, does not detract from its centrality. It remains the flip-side of the coin that Jesus identifies as the true currency of genuine faith. For the Christian, loving others is not an option; it is a command we cannot afford to disobey.

THE REST OF THE STORY

As a whole, the Church has done well teaching people the importance of keeping the first commandment. Our preaching and teaching consistently emphasize the priority of loving the Father. Listening to us, you might even think that Christianity is solely concerned with what goes on between God and isolated, individual human beings.

To such a notion Jesus would surely reply, "Read the rest of the verse." He would confront us, as He did the Pharisees, with the basic imbalance in our understanding of God's will. We who crow so loudly about relating to God may well ignore and abuse His teachings on relating to our neighbor. For which neighbor is a more likely candidate for our affections than the person who sits next to us during Sunday worship? If Jesus calls us to love our neighbors, how much more would He urge us to love our brothers and sisters in Christ? "For anyone who does not love his brother, whom he has seen, cannot love God, whom he has not seen. And he has given us this command: Whoever loves God must also love his brother" (1 John 4:20-21).

Yet it is precisely here that our disobedience becomes most evident. Though the command to love is the same in both instances, we would never think of treating God in many of the ways we routinely treat each other. While preaching passion for God, we commonly settle for apathy toward our brothers and sisters. Loving God means that we trust, respect and serve Him—how often do we act as though loving fellow Christians means no less? As James writes, "With the tongue we praise our Lord and Father, and with it we curse men, who have been made in God's likeness. Out of the same mouth come praise and cursing. My brothers, this should not be" (3:9-10).

In Matthew 18, Jesus told a story that looks a lot like us. A servant who owes his king a great deal of money is called to the throne room. He begs the king to be patient, promising to repay everything. The king has mercy and forgives the man the entire debt. That, of course, is what *our* King has done for each of us. He has forgiven a debt we could not repay. It's easy to love such a generous Master.

How nice it would be if the story had ended with the king's forgiveness, if the servant had lived happily ever after!

It would be comforting to think that religion was just a matter of what goes on in the throne room between us and our forgiving God.

But the practical challenge of Christianity begins with life *outside* the throne room. Like the unmerciful servant in Christ's parable, we often leave the presence of our God who has given us so much only to run into one of our fellow servants who has given us too little. Forgetting how God has treated us, we squeeze our brother's (or sister's) scrawny neck because he owes us some pittance he cannot repay. Jesus ended this parable on a note of judgment to remind all of us that the way we treat each other is just as important as the way we treat God.

It is time for the Church to hear the rest of the story, to read the remainder of the verse, to take seriously the second commandment. Fortunately, the God who intended the Church to be a relationship place did not leave us without an instruction manual. The Bible is filled with practical tools for making local churches gardens where relationships can grow. Page after page encourages us to learn the beautiful art of relating to each other in a godly way. All that needs to be added is a willingness in God's people to look carefully at God's plan for getting back to community and sharing lives personally.

DISCUSSION, REFLECTION, AND ACTION

Chapter Discussion

1. Give everyone a minute to think about the following question: *Think back over your whole life, even your childhood. What has been your best experience of what you think Christian community should be?* Go around the room and let each person describe that experience. Let people pass if

they prefer not to respond. (If your group is meeting for the first time, you want to help people feel comfortable. Be sensitive to all the group members.)

2. a. What do you think the authors mean by calling the Church a "*community* of believers" (page 16)?
   b. Do you agree or disagree with this description? Why?

3. Describe your own experience of community these days. Who is in your community? Who is out of it? How well do you feel it is working?

4. Think about the communities you just discussed in question 3. What things could happen to make you disposable (unneeded) to this community?

5. a. The authors write, "The greatest danger facing the Church today is neither doctrinal nor moral. It is relational" (page 16). Why do they think this?
   b. Do you agree or disagree? Why?

Personal Bible Search
1. Read Luke 10:25-37.
   a. Why did Jesus tell this parable about a good Samaritan?
   b. What point does Jesus make with this parable?
   c. Do you find it easy or hard to act like the good Samaritan? If you find it hard, what are some reasons why?

2. Read Matthew 18:23-35. What lesson about community do you find in this parable?

3. Read James 2:1-9.
   a. What is one way you can break "the royal law" to "love your neighbor as yourself"?

b. How do you think this makes the other person feel?

c. Have you ever seen this happen in a church? If so, describe your experience.

d. How can a church member take steps to avoid doing this?

Personal Reflection and Action

1. a. Think of one person with whom you feel you have a good relationship. What things have you done together this year?

b. Why is doing things together important to relationships?

2. What are you willing to do to make your church more of a community?

3. This week, find a practical way to show love to a neighbor by either:

- forgiving him (Matthew 18:23-35);
- meeting a need (Luke 10:25-37); or
- extending a welcome to a person normally passed over (James 2:1-9).

Plan to tell your group next week about what you did and how the person responded.

CHAPTER TWO

The Urge to Merge

In 1945 social scientist Rene Spitz published a study of infants separated from their mothers and placed in an institutional setting.[1] Most of the children in this study came to the orphanage in relatively good health. In a short time, however, they began to exhibit listlessness, apathy, loss of appetite, and a lack of interest in playthings and other children. If the infants were returned to their mothers, the symptoms disappeared. If on the the other hand the separation continued, the infants deteriorated physically and mentally.

Of twenty-six children between the ages of 1½ and 2½ years observed by Spitz, only two could say more than a couple of words and only three could walk. Though they received adequate nourishment and medical care, twenty-three out of eighty-eight children at the orphange died during the time Spitz did his research.

His published findings shocked the scientific community and sparked a flurry of studies on the problems of institutionalized children. Researchers checked food supplies. They evaluated the quality of medical care provided by orphanages. They tested for infections and viruses and contaminations. Time and again, these studies confirmed that the children scored lower on IQ tests, suffered retardation in verbal and motor development, and faced an increased risk of health problems and even death.

Just when everyone seemed ready to blame the deaths on some mysterious biological reaction to the separation of the child from his mother, a few scientists began to suggest the problem might rather lie in the absence of what a mother provides. At that time, institutions were understaffed and impersonal. Infants received little stimulation or individual attention. Scientists became convinced that these children were suffering and even dying for lack of love.

As a result, researchers developed a prescription to ensure the normal and healthy development of these children. They were to be picked up, held and talked to for some portion of every waking hour. Nurses were ordered to play with the infants and provide them with toys and playmates. These procedures minimized the developmental differences between institutionalized children and home-reared children and eliminated the terrible mortality rates first reported by Spitz.

This institutional disease has come to be known as the "failure-to-thrive syndrome." Among the very young, the absence of touch and personal caring has serious physical and psychological consequences. Infants can die from a lack of loving.

You may be wondering what the problems of institutionalized children have to do with the condition of God's people today. In fact, there is a clear parallel between the orphanage and many churches. A number of us exhibit all the symptoms of a spiritual failure-to-thrive syndrome. After an initial flurry of growth and zeal, many of us settle into listlessness and apathy. We increasingly confine our Christianity to the building and the pew. We lose our appetite for God's Word and become more vulnerable to spiritual sickness and death.

Like the orphanage, churches periodically call in experts who check the quality of pastoral care, the orthodoxy of doctrine, and the biblical IQ of all members. They program for congregational renewal or restructure the leadership or determine that a stewardship campaign is in order.

In reality, what our congregations may need is a prescription much like the one developed for those unfortunate children: "Every Christian is to be picked up, held and talked to for some portion of every waking hour." If church consultants were as perceptive as sociologists, they might decide that many Christians are suffering and even dying from a lack of love.

Unfortunately, some of us are not convinced that loving relationships among Christian people are really that necessary. Say "Hello" to a not-so-rare breed of modern Christian—we'll call him "Robinson Crusoe" because, like the character in Daniel Defoe's novel, he can function fairly well on his own. Robinson is a self-made man, self-sufficient and self-reliant. While in weaker moments he confesses his need for God, you never hear him admit a need for others. He attends church, he gives his money, he even serves on a committee or two. But Robinson is uncomfortable with any call for deeper relationships in the community of Christ. He has been hurt by relationships in the past and is determined to avoid such pain in the future. He smiles at you during worship but is determined to keep his distance.

If Robinson read this chapter he would say, "I am an adult, not a child. I don't need to be cuddled to get along in life. Sure, loving relationships may be *preferable,* but they aren't essential for spiritual health. When I'm feeling a little down, I just pray more or read my Bible. I don't *need* other people to remain faithful to God."

Let's hope he keeps reading. The truth is that God did not design us to go it alone. Even if we could survive spiritually without close association with other Christians, many Christians will not survive without us. Christians need other Christians. If we would look deeper into ourselves, we could see how important relationships are to us. And if we would look deeper into the Bible, we could discover why distinctly Christian relationships are indispensable.

THE SOCIAL ANIMAL

Take a moment and write down your answers to the following questions:

What is the most important thing in your life?

What is the second most important thing in your life?

What is the third most important thing in your life?

When asked to list what is most important to them, people usually answer in terms of relationships. So let's guess that you listed people rather than things as being most important to you. You may have put names beside each question or responded with something like "My marriage," or "Friendship." You probably answered "God" to the first question.

Whatever your responses, they likely have more to do with relationships than with position or pleasure or possessions. Relationships define the truly important things in our lives. They are what we really care about. This is true of all kinds of people, not just those of us who go to church. *Playboy* magazine published a "Poll of American Men" in which readers were asked to indicate what was most important to them.[2] Now picture this. Here is a balding, overweight man with a beer in one hand and pornography in the other, trying to decide what is most important to him. How does he respond? "Miss January"? No. The results of this poll show that even *Playboy* readers rate "Family" and "Friends" at the top of the list.

The old song is wrong when it says, "People who need people are the luckiest people in the world." Such folks are the only people in the world. The Beatles struck closer to the truth when they sang, "All you need is love."

The reason we value relationships lies in the fact that God made us to be social creatures. Our need for others is rooted deeply in the way God designed the human race. That lesson is clearly taught in the Genesis account of Creation.

Seven times in the first chapter, God looked at what He had made and said, "It is good." From the light to the land to the sea creatures—each time He made something, He expressed pleasure over His creation. But in chapter two, God saw something that was not good. He looked at Adam sitting by himself and said, "It is not good that man should be alone" (Genesis 2:18).

Alone. What a terrible word. What pictures of isolation and longing it conjures. Each of us has experienced enough of aloneness that our hearts cry out with God's—it is not good for any one of us to be alone.

But was Adam really alone?

After all, he had a relationship with nature. More than any human being who has come after him, Adam had a relationship with the diverse and wonderful world God made. The plants, the trees, the animals—Adam was on a first-name basis with them all.

Most importantly, however, Adam had a relationship

with God. More than any other character in the divine drama (with the certain exception of Jesus and the possible exception of Moses), Adam enjoyed intimacy with God. The book of Genesis draws the picture of God and Adam walking and talking in the garden, face to face, one on one, together.

Yet it wasn't enough. Something was still missing. In spite of his relationship with nature and the closeness of his walk with God, Adam was still alone. When God looked at him in the garden, He knew Adam was missing the one relationship he needed to make him complete.

It is here that God hit upon the perfect solution to Adam's aloneness. And if you watch closely, it is here we learn something profound about human nature.

> So the Lord God caused the man to fall into a deep
> sleep; and while he was sleeping, he took one of the
> man's ribs and closed up the place with flesh. Then
> the Lord God made a woman from the rib he had
> taken out of the man, and he brought her to the man.
> (Genesis 2:21-22)

When God went searching for a remedy to aloneness, He did not prescribe for Adam a deeper relationship with the environment or even with his God. He gave Adam another human being: "This is bone of my bones and flesh of my flesh!" Only someone made of the same "stuff" as Adam would be capable of achieving the kind of intimacy he required. Had Eve not been taken from Adam's rib, she would not have been able to capture his heart.

Though it is obviously the marriage bond which is the focus of this Genesis passage, a broader lesson can be learned as well. God created us as social animals. Something about us is incomplete without warm, caring, intimate relationships with other human beings. We become unfit for God's purposes when isolated from other people.

Additional threads run through the Bible that lead us to this same conclusion. Have you ever noticed that God has always been in the business of forming groups? First He brought Adam and Eve together, instituting the family. Later, He adopted a nomadic tribe of shepherds as His "special people," establishing the nation of Israel. Finally, He brought together those who confessed faith in Christ, producing the Church.

Though God often worked through individuals, He did so to benefit and further the welfare of His groups. The Old Testament is not so concerned with Moses or David as it is with God's chosen *nation*. The New Testament tells us a great deal about Peter and Paul, but it does so primarily to inform us about the beginnings of God's *Church*. Neither Testament overlooks the importance of the individual; each simply stresses that God is more interested in conducting a symphony than in playing a duet. Over and over we see that God's focus is on people in community.

Though the Bible may not contain a precise psychological explanation of the benefits of relationships, it is full of object lessons that underscore the point that they are important. People who loved and respected each other accomplished tasks that no individual could have done alone. Noah and his sons built an ark; David and his people built a kingdom; Nehemiah and the exiles rebuilt Jerusalem; Jesus and His friends (John 15:15) built the Church.

Notice the examples of close relationships in the Bible: Abraham and Isaac, Jacob and Rachel, Joseph and Benjamin, David and Jonathan, Ruth and Naomi, Esther and Mordecai, Jesus and the Twelve, Paul and Timothy. Each relationship was a tool God used to accomplish His will on earth. Moses had Aaron. Samuel had Eli. Elijah had Elisha. It wasn't by accident that Jesus sent out His disciples to preach "two by two" (Mark 6:7). While other religions venerate their hermits, Jehovah has never had much use for loners.

Note also the Bible's emphasis on the devastation that broken relationships bring: Cain's envy of Abel, the hatred between Jacob and Esau, the jealousy of Joseph's brothers, Saul's anger towards David, David's betrayal of Uriah, the treachery of Judas, the ill feelings between Euodia and Syntyche. God used each case to highlight the seriousness of treating others right and the terrible consequences that result when we fail to do so.

This emphasis on community and friendship and relationships is rooted in Creation and in the way God made us. We are relationship creatures. This is the environment for which God designed us. Right relationships strengthen us and further God's Kingdom; broken relationships stunt us and stymie God's plans. That is the consistent message of His Word. It is not good for man to be alone.

Solomon said it best when he wrote:

Two are better than one,
    because they have a good return for their work:
If one falls down, his friend can help him up.
But pity the man who falls
    and has no one to help him up!
Also, if two lie down together, they will keep warm.
    But how can one keep warm alone?
Though one may be overpowered,
    two can defend themselves.
A cord of three strands is not quickly broken.

                              (Ecclesiastes 4:9-12)

People need people. Only within the presence of others do we truly become what God created us to be—and that principle holds whether we sit naked in the Garden of

Eden or dressed in a three-piece suit in New York City. A human being is not really human unless he is plural.

BY HOOK OR BY CROOK

Individuals go to extraordinary lengths to meet their needs. The body, for example, needs oxygen. Losing our supply of air threatens our very lives. Time and energy go into meeting this need from the moment we are born.

Proper breathing, however, always requires a proper atmosphere. All the breathing in the world won't make up for the wrong environment. Take, for instance, a person who is drowning. A drowning victim does not die because he refuses to breathe; he dies because he tries to breathe in the wrong environment. He may hold his breath for a while, but when unconsciousness comes, the body ignores the environment and expands its lungs in a desperate attempt to meet its need.

With that effort the body dooms itself. For though it fights to meet a legitimate need, it does so in an inappropriate environment. The body dies, not for lack of breathing but for lack of atmosphere.

That's the way it is with needs. We do everything in our power to meet them appropriately. When that is not possible, however, we desperately attempt to meet them even in the wrong environments. By hook or by crook, appropriately or inappropriately, in right ways or in wrong, needs *will* be met—or else we die trying!

The same is true with our need for relationship. We require love as part of the way God made us. As the body is made for oxygen, so the soul is made for relationship. Children who fail to thrive physically in the absence of touch and stimulation are not so different from adults who fail to thrive spiritually and emotionally without caring relationships. Both need what love offers. The God who declared Adam unsuited to go it alone declares the same about us today. If we refuse relationship, we go not only against our own nature, but against our Creator.

But proper relationships also require a proper atmosphere. In some environments, this need to love and be loved can be met appropriately—places where we can breathe deeply of the caring and warmth necessary to our existence. God, who created our need for love, has also created places (like the home and the Church) where this need can be met. If these environments function as they should, we have a never-ending source of fresh and rejuvenating relationships with which to feed our souls.

When these appropriate environments fail to function as God designed them, people turn to other surroundings to meet their need for relationship. A bar, an illicit affair, a cult—each seduces its victims with promises of closer fellowship than they found in God's relationship places. When the proper and God-given climates for intimacy become unfulfilling and stagnant, people attempt in desperation to breathe in an environment for which they were not designed.

And they die.

Like all needs, the need to love and be loved will be met. Rightly or wrongly, in good ways or in bad, everyone finds an atmosphere where this need can be met. And though that search may end in frustration and emotional death, it won't be because people refused to search for real relationships. More likely, failure will result because they searched hard, but in all the wrong places.

Meanwhile, Christians can piously condemn the world's attempts to find relationship. We can post "Danger!" signs at every bottomless pit that promises love but delivers death. We can lament every brother or sister who leaves God's relationship place for the tempting pool in Satan's backyard. And we can mourn over those who continue to drown because they are trapped in an environment for which they were not designed.

Perhaps our efforts would be better spent making God's relationship place the kind of environment that is not only appropriate but *satisfying* as well. If we did a better job in our homes and churches of meeting the need for relationship, perhaps so many would not pass our door on their way to Satan's place.

People will find some way to meet their need for relationship. It is up to us to make sure that God's environment will be that place.

DISCUSSION, REFLECTION, AND ACTION

Chapter Discussion

1. Recall one incident from when you were in junior high school that has either made it *easier* or *harder* for you to open up and relate to people. Share this with your group or one other person.

2. The authors describe how babies fail to thrive unless they are held and talked to. How have you been "picked up and talked to" during the past week?

3. a. If you haven't already done so, write down your answers to the questions on page 28. Then share your answers with your group.
   b. What do your answers tell you about yourself and your needs?
   c. What do other group members' answers tell you about them?

4. a. In what kinds of nonChristian environments are people you know trying to meet their needs?

b. How well are they succeeding at meeting their needs in those environments? What is happening to them?

5. What good things do you think can occur when church members decide to "play in God's symphony" rather than "play solos"?

Personal Bible Search

1. Read Matthew 4:18-22.
   a. What was the first thing Jesus did as He began His public ministry?
   b. Why do you think He did this?

2. Read 1 Kings 19:1-18.
   a. What were the circumstances that made Elijah upset?
   b. What was the first question God asked him (19:9)?
   c. Why do you think God asked that particular question?
   d. How did God encourage Elijah to get involved again with the people and ministry he had left?
   e. What lessons does this story offer us when we are tempted to give up on relationships in the Church?

3. Read Hebrews 10:24-25.
   a. What are the purposes of assembling with other believers?
   b. How can you put what this passage says into practice?

Personal Reflection and Action

1. How can close relationships help you in your commitment to Jesus?

2. What kinds of things have you done in order to get

acceptance? Which were good, and which were bad methods? Which had good results, and which had bad ones? What do you think you should have done differently?

3. Describe a time during the past month when you really felt good about something. Did it have to do with a relationship?

CHAPTER THREE

God's Relationship Place

One of the most popular television shows of recent years has been the bawdy and ribald comedy "Cheers." Set in a Boston tavern, the series revolves around the patrons who frequent the bar. No murders or kidnappings, no high-speed chase scenes, no drug deals or criminal conspiracies— just the interactions of lonely people who are drawn to the camaraderie of crying in one another's beer.

While you may not appreciate the humor of the show, it is important to appreciate the reason for the show's popularity. The theme song outlines the basis for this comedy's plot and says much in explanation of its enduring success:

> Making your way in the world today
>   takes everything you've got.
> Taking a break from all your worries
>   sure would help a lot.
> Wouldn't you like to get away?
>
> Sometimes you wanna go
>   where everybody knows your name,
>   and they're always glad you came.
> You wanna be where you can see

our troubles are all the same.
You wanna go where everybody knows your name.[1]

The characters of "Cheers" are greeted heartily when they enter the tavern. Their friends make a place for them at the bar and ask about their day. They share their doubts and fears, their failures and victories, their hates and loves. This is group therapy for the price of a six-pack, confession without a priest, acceptance without fear of rejection. Millions tune in each week to experience a vicarious belonging and—at some level of consciousness—must wonder if there might be such a place for them.

Some smart producer recognized what many Christians fail to see: People are looking for a place where they are known, where others are glad to see them, where they are accepted and called by name. They search for an environment where their need to love and be loved can be met, where they can connect with others and breathe the heady perfume of relationship. They are not picky about where they find this environment—they know beggars can't be choosers.

Does the God who made us "relationship creatures" provide an alternative to the bars, clubs, and other gathering places of the world? Wouldn't the One who created our need for others also create an appropriate environment for that need to be met? By God's design, fish swim in schools, wolves roam in packs, bees fly in swarms. Quail covey, cattle herd, geese gaggle. What do *people* do when they gather to support, nourish, and protect each other in appropriate and godly groupings? In a word, they *church!*

WHAT IS THE CHURCH?

When you think about the "Church," what images come to mind? Many people see the Church as a *lecture hall*—a place to go to hear the Bible taught. Others view the Church as a *theater*—a place to watch the drama of Christ reenacted. Still others think of the Church as a *corporation*—a program-oriented retail chain for marketing religion to the masses. A growing number of people look at the Church as a *social club*—a place to exchange niceties, enjoy congenial conversations, and make social contacts.

The common denominator of all these definitions is that they see the Church as an "it," a place or thing, an entity unto itself. The people of the Church are somehow distinct from the Church itself. They are observers or listeners or customers or patients. But they are not the Church. Christians may "go to church" or "give to a church" or "build a church," but seem uncomfortable with the notion, *"We are the Church."* In the thinking of many of us, the Church is bigger than the people in the pews.

It appears that many Christians define the Church *structurally,* seeing it more as a corporation than as a community. They identify certain characteristics of the true Church and define the Church exclusively in those terms. How should the Church be organized? What are the proper modes of worship? What are the specific terms of membership? What are the tasks the Church is responsible to perform? These issues have consumed our thinking and have shaped the way we define "Church." Almost unconsciously, we view the Church from an organizational, programmatic, and structural perspective.

Such a view is not wrong. The New Testament itself speaks of the Church from this perspective. Matthew 16:13-18 defines the Church as a confessing entity. First Corinthians 14:26-40 refers to the Church as a worshiping entity. First Timothy 3:1-13 and Titus 1:5-9 clearly teach the Church is an organizational entity.

We have gone wrong not because we see the Church in

structural terms but because we have tended to do so exclusively. Understanding the Church in its worshiping, organizational, and teaching capacity, many of us feel we have plumbed the depths of the Bible's portrayal of this subject. Unfortunately, that is simply not the case.

You know of congregations that teach all the correct doctrines, organize according to biblical precedents, and worship decently and in order (1 Corinthians 14:40)—yet they are as dead as the buildings in which they meet. There is no discernible moving of the Spirit, no excitement or joy or growth. There is a great deal of correctness before God but little spontaneity—lots of structure but no life.

Such congregations face the same predicament as Dr. Frankenstein. He too had assembled all the necessary pieces and meticulously sewn them together. There lay his monster, structurally and anatomically correct. Yet the creature was lifeless. For Frankenstein to create life, he needed something more than a corpse—he needed a catalyst. Even the mad scientist knew when it was time to stop looking for limbs and start looking for lightning!

The Church also needs a catalyst to make the transition from organization to organism. Certainly a number of dynamics make the Church a living and breathing entity— faith in the risen Christ and individual commitment, to name but two. As we search for the lightning that will bring churches to life, however, we must not overlook the significance of relationships.

The hard reality is that the Church is much more than its programs or teachings or structures. There is a *relational* component to God's vision of the Church that breathes life into the Bride of Christ.

God never intended the Church to be primarily a "worshiping place" or an organization through which He could accomplish certain tasks. God's view of the Church has always included the notion of a gathering of people—an assembly convened for fellowship, support, encouragement, and love. God, who designed men and women as relationship creatures, designed the Church as a "relationship place"—the environment in which people could find the best answers for their need to love and to be loved.

For every New Testament passage that speaks of how the Church should be organized, there is another that describes how its members should relate. For every teaching about the *theology* of the Church, there is another on the *sociology* of the Church. As important as it is to know the proper *form* of the Church, it is equally important that we understand its proper *function.*

TOWARDS A BIBLICAL UNDERSTANDING OF "CHURCH"

At least three New Testament images cast the Church in *relational* terms. Though they do not invalidate speaking of the Church as a structural unit, they add a component to our definition of "Church" that cannot be ignored. These pictures are so strong and pervasive that they make us question whether we can ever create a true Church without incorporating relational ideas at the most basic levels of Church life.

THE CHURCH AS BODY

In writing to the Corinthian church, Paul faced some. difficult issues. This group of Christians (like many Christians today) failed to grasp that the Church was a relationship place. They did not understand that the way they treated each other was as important as the purity of their morals or the content of their faith or the quality of their worship. There were divisions among them, lawsuits between them, and ill will all around.

To address these problems, Paul used the word *body* in a way that is peculiarly his. For the first time, he spoke of the *Church* as a body, and with this image pressed home some clear teaching about relationships among Christians.

> The body is a unit, though it is made up of many parts; and though all its parts are many, they form one body. So it is with Christ. For we were all baptized by one Spirit into one body. . . . Now you are the body of Christ, and each one of you is a part of it.
>
> (1 Corinthians 12:12-13,27)

It is impossible to overemphasize the significance of Paul's statement here. We are a body, he said—not *like* a body or *similar* to a body, but we *are* a body. That reality places new meaning on how we view ourselves. We are no longer simply a group who believes alike or works toward a common goal or worships according to a similar pattern. As members of a body, we define ourselves as much by how we relate to one another as by the particular forms we share.

To better understand Paul's analogy, consider this: Most of us think nothing of chewing nervously on a fingernail. We all know a few confirmed nail-biters. Though it is not a habit to be proud of, it is not something we view with disgust or revulsion. But take that same fingernail, clip it from the finger, and *then* chew on it—the thought makes us queasy.

Why the change of attitude? It is the same fingernail, the same mouth, the same taste and consistency. The only difference is our perception of ownership. So long as a fingernail is attached to our finger, it is a part of our bodies, an extension of ourselves. As Paul wrote, "After all, no one ever hated his own body" (Ephesians 5:29).

But as soon as a fingernail is clipped, it becomes something alien to our bodies. No longer a part of ourselves, it does not belong to us as it did just seconds before. And because it is something "other" than us, our attitude toward it alters radically. We no longer manicure it or paint it or chew it affectionately. It is no longer a part of us and is fit only for the nearest garbage can.

When Paul called the Church of Jesus a "body," it makes you wonder if he didn't have a similar idea in mind. So long as members consider each other a part of a body, there is *ownership*. We take care of each other and consider each other an extension of ourselves. We may even chew on each other, but it is with gentleness and affection.

The moment we clip other Christians away from the body, however, they become alien and strange. Since they no longer belong to us, our attitudes toward them alter radically. We don't feel responsible to take care of them and protect them. When former brothers and sisters become so many clippings, we feel justified in throwing them away.

In calling the Church a "body," Paul was stressing a relational component of Church life, something far more significant and meaningful than mere Church structure. The Church for Paul is more than a reservoir of correct answers to theological questions—it is a living, breathing organism made up of members who are connected to and dependent on each other.

THE CHURCH AS FAMILY

The precise date when Christians began to regard one another as "brother" and "sister" is not known. Certainly, the Jews—who all traced their lineage to Abraham— considered one another family. The Old Testament often uses "brother" as a synonymn for "countryman." By the time of Jesus, this usage was so well established that He could use "brother" and "sister" in a much wider context than blood relationship. Thus He could speak of not being angry with a "brother" or the speck in a "brother's eye" without fear of His audience limiting these commands to kin.

On one occasion Jesus made it plain that He had redefined the terms normally reserved for family to include those whose tie to Him was closer than blood. When informed (Matthew 12:47) that His (natural) mother and brothers were waiting for Him, Jesus pointed to His disciples and said, "Here are my mother and my brothers. For whoever does the will of my Father in heaven is my brother and sister and mother."

The early Church took this statement at face value. The epistles are replete with references to "brothers" and "sisters" whose only relation was that established in the Lord. Peter even refers to the Church as a "brotherhood of believers" (1 Peter 2:17), and admonishes Christians to add to godliness the quality of *brotherly* affection (2 Peter 1:7).

It is not surprising, then, that the New Testament refers to the Church as a "family" (*oikos*). Paul encourages the Galatians to "do good to all people, especially to those who belong to the *family* of believers" (6:10, emphasis added). In the Ephesian letter, he welcomes Gentiles into the Church with the words, "you are no longer foreigners and aliens, but fellow citizens with God's people and *members of God's household*" (2:19, emphasis added).

Paul's most striking use of this image is found in 1 Timothy 3:15. He has just finished writing about elders and deacons and the importance of Church leaders managing their own families (*oikos*—3:5,12). He has further described the responsibilities of wives and children in a leader's home. In this context Paul begins to talk about *God's* family, instructing Timothy about "how people ought to conduct themselves in God's household [*oikos*], *which is the church of the living God*" (emphasis added). Paul leaves no doubt that when he thinks of the Church, he thinks of a family, a household, a home in which God dwells.

As with the body image, the New Testament uses the picture of the family to emphasize the relational aspect of Church life. Once again, we are challenged to view ourselves as more than the sum of our dogmas and rituals. We are a community of interrelated people, a caring and fraternal fellowship who define ourselves as much by the closeness of our association as by the content of our message.

THE CHURCH AS FELLOWSHIP

Though there are many other pictures of the Church painted in the hue of relationship, this third image is perhaps the most vivid of them all. The word *koinonia* is sometimes used in the New Testament as a synonym for "Church." It is translated in a variety of ways: "partnership," "participation," "close relationship." The most popular translation of the word, however, is "fellowship."

> [*Koinonos*] implies fellowship or sharing with someone or in something. . . . The main element in *koinonos* is that of fellowship. Hence the word is especially adapted to express inner relationship.[2]

Among the Greeks, "koinonia" was a relationship word. It was a favorite expression for the marital relationship. It described the closeness of friendship and the collaboration of business partners. When the New Testament writers chose "koinonia" to describe the Church, they deliberately chose a word that carried *relational* overtones.

The 3000 who responded to the message of Peter at Pentecost not only were "added to their number" (that is, to the body of believers) but devoted themselves to the fellowship (koinonia—Acts 2:42). When John wrote his first letter, pointing out the differences between those who walk in the light and those who walk in darkness, he began the letter by talking about koinonia: "We proclaim to you what we have seen and heard, so that you also may have *fellowship* with us. And our *fellowship* is with the Father and with his Son, Jesus Christ" (1 John 1:3). Paul and Barnabas traveled to Jerusalem with the story of their ministry among the Gentiles; there James, Peter and John extended to them the "right hand of fellowship" (koinonia—Galatians 2:9).

In each case, it is not "fellowshiping" (the verb form) that is stressed, but "fellowship" (the noun)—not what the Church does so much as what the Church is. In one of those strange twists of language, an activity of the Church comes to symbolize the Church as a whole, and helps to define an important aspect of the New Testament Church.

It is difficult if not impossible to limit "fellowship" to structural matters. "*Koinonia* is the quality of relationship where a person belongs, not because of particular skills or contributions, but for no other reason than that here is a child of God."[3] By definition, the term insists that when we think of the Church as a fellowship, we think primarily of the Church from a relational perspective. If in fact the New Testament portrays the Church as a "partnership," a "communion," a "mutual sharing," we do damage to God's understanding of "Church" when we think of it in purely structural terms.

"LORD, MAKE US MORE LIKE A TAVERN!"

Churches are often completely blind to the necessity of being a body or a family or a fellowship. It is enough that they be structurally precise, that their doctrines be in order, and that the doors of the building be open for the ceremony and ritual of the Church. The fact that their pews hold lonely, alienated people is of little concern. That they more closely resemble a classroom than a family is to them somehow beside the point.

But is it *really* beside the point? Can we be Christ's true Church without also having a vibrant fellowship and a strong sense of community? Even if we know all the correct answers, hold firm to the faith of our fathers, and worship only in accordance with the biblical pattern—if we are not a loving community where people can find acceptance and friendship and compassion, can we really call ourselves the Church?

The world hungers to meet its need to love and be loved. People search for an environment where relationships can blossom. Though they may not even believe in the God who made them relational creatures, they are nonetheless driven to meet the needs with which their Creator endowed them. By hook or by crook, in good ways or in bad, our friends and neighbors will fight their aloneness—or die trying.

When the Church functions as it should, the world has a place to turn where those needs can be met. As a relationship place—a body/family/fellowship—the Church offers its most compelling and attractive face to the world. But when the Church fails to function relationally, it shouldn't surprise us that the world turns elsewhere to find its relationship fix. The choice between staying in the Church and starving to death emotionally or turning to other environments that at least promise the warmth we need is really no choice at all.

Satan has not overlooked our failure to make the Church an environment where fellowship flourishes. Always the lion in search of prey, Satan has set out a wide variety of people traps—attractive cages baited with pseudo-intimacy and plastic passions. He offers an imitation of what should be the Church's reality. Unfortunately, in the absence of the real thing, many have found the substitute too appealing to resist. For example:

> The neighborhood bar is possibly the best counterfeit that there is to the fellowship Christ wants to give his Church. It's an imitation, dispensing liquor instead of grace, escape rather than reality—but it is a permissive, accepting, and inclusive fellowship. It is unshockable. It is democratic. You can tell people secrets, and they usually don't tell others or even want to. The bar flourishes not because most people are alcoholics, but because God has put into the human heart the desire to know and be known, to love and be loved, and so many seek a counterfeit at the price of a few beers. With all my heart, I believe that Christ wants his church to be unshockable, a fellowship where people can come in and say, I'm sunk, I'm beat, I've had it. Alcoholics Anonymous has this quality— our churches too often miss it.[4]

If the Church today is missing this quality, it is fair to note that the Church of the first century was not. Our New Testaments reveal closer parallels between the early Church and the modern tavern than between it and the stained glass churches of today. Perhaps our prayer ought to be, "Lord, make the Church more like a tavern."

As Christian people we have a choice to make. We can either make the Church a relationship place where the need to love and be loved can be met, or we can watch the world continue to walk past our buildings to other environments that will surely kill them in the end.

DISCUSSION, REFLECTION, AND ACTION

Chapter Discussion

1. Do you find the place described in the *Cheers* theme song attractive? If so, what is attractive to you about it?

2. To what extent do the words of this song describe your church or small group? (Try to be honest with your group about how well you think it fulfills what the song describes.)

3. a. What makes individual members—a hand, an eye, an ear—into a body? (See 1 Corinthians 12:18.)
   b. What makes bricks and mortar into a building?
   c. What makes offspring into a family?

4. The authors say, "It is difficult, if not impossible, to describe fellowship in a structural manner." Do you agree or disagree? Why?

5. a. What was your first reaction to the prayer on page 50, "Lord, make the Church more like a tavern"?
   b. What is your current reaction?
   c. What do you think the authors are saying in this prayer?

Personal Bible Search

1. Read Acts 2:42-47.
   a. What contributed to the warm fellowship of this first church?
   b. What was the result of this unity?

2. Read Ephesians 4:1-6.
   a. How does the Church live "worthy of its calling"?
   b. What kinds of "effort" must be put forth if the "unity of the Spirit" is to be kept?

c. Study the seven "ones" that are to be in the Church. What does each mean? What are the implications for your life?

3. Read 1 John 1:1-4.
   a. Why does John proclaim what he has "seen and heard"?
   b. Kenneth Mitchell is quoted on page 48: "*Koinonia* is the quality of relationship where a person belongs . . . for no other reason than that here is a child of God." How does this statement agree or disagree with the latter part of 1 John 1:3?

Personal Reflection and Action
1. Describe your impression of the last Christian group you encountered outside your own church.

2. Evaluate your own church or group as a body, a family, and a fellowship. How can you help make your church more of a relationship place?

3. a. What have you done in groups that has brought you closer to members of that group? Make a list.
   b. Select one or two activities from your list, and do them with others in your church or group this week.

CHAPTER FOUR

Will the Real Christian Please Stand?

"Hurry! Hurry! Step right up! Ladies and Gentlemen, prepare to be amazed and shocked. You are about to witness one of the true wonders of the world—a human being so different from you and me it will make your head spin. This is not a sight for the queasy or the weak, but if you can stand it, you'll be telling your grandkids what you've seen tonight. Without further ado, let me present to you THE CHRISTIAN!!!" [*The curtain goes up, revealing a particularly graphic example of this strange creature, to the accompaniment of many oohs and ahhs. Women gather their children and hurry away. Not a few of the men look decidedly pale.*]

Something not unlike this has been going on in the news media during recent years. A handsome, well-dressed journalist parades the latest example of Christian failure before millions of viewers who, in turn, respond with the proper mixture of amazement, disdain, and revulsion.

You probably knew what was coming before the reporter opened his mouth. You've seen the show. On stage is an overdressed, jewelry embellished huckster spreading one minute of gospel among twenty-nine minutes of fundraising appeals. Or perhaps the victim is a renowned minister whom clever reporters have unmasked as a weak and sinful human after all. Most pathetic of all are the pictures of political zealots killing each other under the unfortunate labels of Catholic and Protestant, presumably for the greater glory of God. Whatever the episode, the message we hear is clear: With Christians like these, who needs infidels?

It's time to fight fire with fire. Since this is the age of mass media, and since it is being used so effectively against us, it seems only fair that we employ the methods of the advertisers to let the world know there are some decent Christians left.

The world needs a way to identify genuine Christians. We could take out full-page advertisements in the newspapers of our cities and buy local or even national time on the tube. We should hire a Madison Avenue advertising agency to design a campaign to rival the slickest beer promotions. We shall spare no expense or effort to sell the message that we are the TRUE Christians with the TRUE answers to the TRUE issues of life.

Besides all that advertising, we'll agree on a logo, something to identify us personally with the media blitz. Those of us unashamed of our faith really need some type of lapel pin—maybe in the shape of a fish or embossed with the name "Jesus." We could put them right on our coats or dresses—or hey, even on our cars—so that people would realize, "Oh, so *you're* a Christian. Wow—I saw your commercial on TV. How did they get Spuds McKenzie to pound a Bible like that?"

Of course, any adman sporting a power tie knows that you have to get people's attention before they'll listen to what you have to say. Maybe on top of everything else Christians should try a little strangeness. We could dress eccentrically and wear white robes instead of business suits. It works for the Hari Krishnas; maybe it would work for us.

No, no—you're right—perhaps that's going a bit far. Why don't we just *talk* strangely, then? If we use a lot of Christianese and speak in language forms nobody in our culture has heard for the last three hundred years, that would do the trick. Yeah. That's it.

BY *THIS* THEY WILL KNOW

Do these and other desperate strategies ever dart through your mind? What in the world *can* we do to communicate to the world we are the people of Jesus Christ? The only thing more damning to the Christian than being ridiculed is being ignored. We are supposed to be the "salt of the earth" and the "light of the world." Salt and light are intended to be noticed, and so are Christians. How can we go into all the world and preach the gospel if nobody pays any attention to us when we get there?

It shouldn't surprise us that the One who told us to be salt and light also gave us the strategy by which we would be noticed.

> A new command I give you: Love one another. As I have loved you, so you must love one another. By this all men will know that you are my disciples, if you love one another.   (John 13:34-35)

"Everyone will know who you are," says Jesus, "if you love each other." The importance of love we have already examined from a number of angles: its significance for us as individuals, and its place in the life of the Church. But love plays an even bigger role in God's design. By gaining insight into this passage, we can begin to understand the role love plays not only for the individual and the Church, but as a sign for the entire world.

Jesus insists love is the mark which witnesses to the world of the identity and authenticity of His followers. If we need a means of showing the world we are genuine Christians, perhaps this would be a good place to begin.

LOVE IS A COMMAND[1]

A new command I give you: Love one another.

(John 13:34).

Within the pages of the Bible are many commands, but few of them are prefaced by a flashing light for emphasis. This one is. "Here comes a command," Jesus warns. "It may sound new, but it is still God's will."

Loving our brothers and sisters is an edict as binding as "Thou shalt not steal" or "Honor thy father and thy mother" or any other command. It is just as important as modes of worship or matters of doctrine or standards of morality.

Jesus contended, in fact, that some precepts were more important than others. It could be argued that this command carries greater weight than many. Jesus Himself certainly gave it high priority, ranking it second only to the command to love our God.

Loving each other is a command, not an option for Christians. Since Jesus commanded love, it is not a responsibility we can afford to regard lightly. The world may call a lack of warm and loving relationships "self-sufficiency." In the Church, such detachment has another designation—
disobedience.

LOVE IS A *DIFFICULT* COMMAND

As I have loved you, so you must love one another.

(John 13:34)

Don't you wish Jesus had quit after the first part of verse 34? "A new commandment I give to you: love one another." If He had put a period there and not followed on with the rest of verse 34, we would be so much better off. Well, at least things would be easier.

Jesus could simply have commanded us to love each other and then allowed us to guess what He meant by that. How might we have defined "love"? Would we be tempted to interpret love as some watered down, diluted, ecumenical togetherness? If we see each other on Sunday mornings—then we love each other! If we speak civilly and get along fairly well—we must surely love each other! If we don't shout and scream and rant—that must be the proof of our love for each other! Left to our own definitions, love would quickly depreciate into something far from what Jesus intended.

But Christ did not leave the defining to us. He said, "Love each other *as I have loved you.*" Jesus was not just telling us we *ought* to love; He was telling us *how much.*

Do you see why this is called a *difficult* command? Jesus insists here that the way Christians treat each other must be the same way He treats us. We are commanded to love each other. But more to the point, we are commanded to love as *Jesus* loved.

What images does that bring to mind? Do you think of Jesus' patience in dealing with Peter? Do you remember His tenderness with the woman caught in adultery? Can you picture Him washing the traitor's feet? That's how Jesus loves us.

Look at His bloodied back. Notice the crown of thorns. Place your fingers in the nail prints and feel the roughness of the cross. That's how Jesus loves us. All this and more is the way Jesus commands us to love each other.

That's hard, but it's still not optional. If we are to be

obedient followers of Jesus Christ, we must start loving each other as He has loved us.

LOVE IS A *DISTINCTLY* DIFFICULT COMMAND

By this all men will know that you are my disciples if you love one another. (John 13:35)

Here is the answer to the question, "How will the world know we are Christians?" "They'll know you are Mine," Jesus says, "when you show a love like Mine." Christ's difficult love is the mark of true discipleship.

It's not the symbols we wear or the type of clothing we use. It's not the advertising we do. What communicates to the world that we are the people of God is our Christlike treatment of people.

It is amazing that Jesus would insist only *one* thing best communicates to the world that we are His disciples. He didn't single out our stand on a particular issue, or the way we organize our churches, or even our commitment to the authority of the Bible as the distinguishing characteristic of the disciple. *One* thing Jesus points out as being the mark of the Christian for the world, and that is our love for one another. There may be additional marks the Church must use internally to distinguish the sheep from the goats (obedience and doctrine, for example), but as Francis Schaeffer wrote:

> [We] cannot expect the world to judge that way, because the world cares nothing about doctrine. . . . If we are surrounded by a world which no longer believes in the concept of truth, certainly we cannot expect people to have any interest in whether a man's doctrine is correct or not.

But Jesus did give the mark that will arrest the attention of the world. . . . What is it? The love that true Christians show for each other.[2]

The Church of Christ will bear the mark of Christ when we start loving as Christ loved. That kind of love is a *distinct* love. It's a love that is different from anything else the world has ever seen—except in Jesus of Nazareth.

When the world looks at Jesus' love it sits in amazement, shocked by what it sees. It cannot understand a love which prays for its enemies, as Jesus did for the Roman soldiers who crucified Him. It cannot understand a love which embraces a nobody, as Jesus did with the thief crucified beside Him. It cannot understand a love which gives people "70 times 7" chances, as Jesus did with Simon Peter and required him to do for others. It cannot understand a love which gives without expecting repayment, returns good for evil, goes the second mile, and touches the leper.

Though nonbelievers may not understand such love, they certainly appreciate it when they see it. Christ's contemporaries marveled at His treatment of people. Whether it was a woman by a well in Samaria or a sinner weeping at His feet in Simon's house or a former maniac in the region of the Gadarenes, they all experienced a kind of love they had never known before. A transforming love. A love that touched lives.

If that love was striking in Jesus' day, it will be in ours as well. People haven't changed that much. If anything, the hunger to see a Christlike love has grown more acute. As people in our society drift further from one another, as trust dies and suspicion builds, people will be more and more attracted to a community of people that behaves as family, that comes to the aid of its members, that treats each individual as a valued part of the whole.

Recently a deacon in the Lincoln Church lost his wife after a two-year battle with cancer. During that long illness, there were young children to care for, meals to make, a house to clean. The congregation rallied around this family. Two couples provided much of the childcare for several months. The church paid for a professional maid service to clean the house weekly. Members brought daily meals to the home, and some traveled hundreds of miles to sit with the husband while his wife underwent surgery. There were calls and cards and prayer sessions.

After the funeral the husband's boss took the preacher aside. "I want to tell you something," he confided. "I have never seen anything like what this church has done for this family. I can't get over the kind of support and love you have shown. It's the most amazing display of Christian charity I have ever witnessed." He went on and on until finally the preacher had to excuse himself to minister to other mourners. At that point the man found another member of the church and repeated the whole thing again!

When we start loving each other as Jesus has loved us, the world notices. Our friends and fellow workers and neighbors recognize something in us that convicts them and causes them to say, "Those people have been with Jesus."

So what does the world see in us? What are we known for? The unbelieving people around you are hungry to see that you bear the mark of the Christian. They don't want clever advertising or lapel pins or strangeness. They want to see relationships that give them hope that love has not died. They are starving to see living examples of the trust, commitment, and caring their own relationships lack. They want proof that in a world where relationships are disposable it is still possible to treat people as if they genuinely matter. When they can see Christians treating each other that way, they eagerly listen to anything we have to say.

If you look too closely at Church history you might think Christians were known more for their fighting than for their loving. Someone may say, "Yes, but we argue and split because of our love for truth!"

Christians should love God's truth. But any person or any group of people who sacrifices love for the sake of truth *has lost the truth!* There is no greater truth than love.

This is not to say that other doctrines or biblical principles are unimportant. It is to affirm the words of the Apostle Paul:

> If I have the gift of prophecy and can fathom all mysteries and all knowledge, and if I have a faith that can move mountains, but have not love, I am *nothing.*
>
> (1 Corinthians 13:2)

A sad reality shows in Christians worn out by biting and devouring each other over religious issues. Even when all of the issues have been hammered out and firm conclusions have been reached on every question, no one is left to listen to the answers. Why should our neighbors care about our hard-won doctrinal positions when they have not seen those positions make a difference in how we treat each other? They won't care what we teach if they haven't seen Christ's love in the way we live.

What is the mark of the Christian? What is it that tells everyone watching that we are the people of Jesus Christ? It is Christians living a Christlike love:

> The Christians know and trust their God. They placate those who oppress them and make their enemies their friends. They do good to their enemies. Their wives are absolutely pure and their daughters are

modest. Their men abstain from unlawful marriages, and all other impurity.

If any of them have bondwomen or children, they persuade them to become Christians for the love they have toward them; and when they become so, they call them "brother" without distinction. They love one another.

They rescue the orphan from him who does him violence. He who has gives ungrudgingly to him that has not. If they see a stranger, they take him into their dwellings and rejoice over him as over a real brother; for they do not call each other brother after the flesh, but after the Spirit of God. If any among them is poor and needy, and they do not have food to spare, they fast two or three days that they may supply him with necessary food.

But, the deeds which they do, they do not proclaim to the ears of the multitude, but they take care that no man shall perceive them. Thus they labor to become righteous. Truly, this is a new people and there is something divine in them.

Letter written to the
Roman Emperor Hadrian
(AD 117-138)

DISCUSSION, REFLECTION, AND ACTION

Chapter Discussion

1. a. On page 54 the authors state, "With Christians like these, who needs infidels?" Why do you think the authors make this statement?

   b. Do you think this statement is too harsh or too soft? Why or why not?

2. Recall the last time a nonChristian rejected you for being a Christian. What do you think he or she was really rejecting?

3. In John 13:34-35, Jesus commands us to love each other. How can love be commanded?

4. a. What does "as I have loved you" tell you about the meaning of love?
   b. Why is this crucial to your understanding of love?

5. Describe some examples of love you have seen. How have they affected you and others?

Personal Bible Search
1. Read 1 Corinthians 6:1-11.
   a. What were the Corinthians doing that upset Paul?
   b. Why was this so damaging to their witness for Christ?
   c. If a situation like this continues to exist in a church, who is the real winner? Who is the real loser?
   d. Paul reminded the Corinthians that they had been washed, sanctified, and justified in the name of Jesus and by the Spirit of God (6:11). How should these facts have affected the way they treated each other?

2. Read Luke 3:12-14.
   a. John the Baptist was approached by two kinds of seekers. What did each group ask?
   b. How did John respond to each group?
   c. What does this tell you about the fruit of a repentant life?

3. Read Galatians 5:13-15.
   a. What does the Galatians' freedom give them a chance to do?

b. Why do you think the law can be summed up in the statement, "Love your neighbor as yourself"?

c. What does 5:15 say about the way we treat each other in the church today?

Personal Reflection and Action

1. In what three ways can you exhibit in your family the love Jesus describes in John 13:34-35?

2. In what three ways can you do this in your church?

3. Is it realistic to think that you can exhibit both the love of God and the holiness of God simultaneously? Why or why not?

CHAPTER FIVE

What Is Love?

"I don't know what you mean by 'glory,'" Alice said.

Humpty Dumpty smiled contemptuously. "Of course you don't—till I tell you. I meant 'there's a nice knock-down argument for you!'"

"But 'glory' doesn't mean a 'nice knock-down argument,'" Alice objected.

"When I use a word," Humpty Dumpty said, in rather a scornful tone, "it means just what I choose it to mean—neither more nor less."

"The question is," said Alice, "whether you can make words mean so many different things."

"The question is," said Humpty Dumpty, "which is to be master—that's all."

Lewis Carroll
Through the Looking Glass

Let us go down and there confound their languáge, that they may not understand one another's speech.
(Genesis 11:7)

What meaning do *you* attach to the word *love?* Some of us think of love as syrupy sentimentalism—an overly-sweet, touchy-feely form of relating that makes no demands. It has no backbone. Others think primarily of "tough love"—the willingness to discipline and correct those we truly cherish. Still others define love as the absence of malice and resentment. One young woman, certain she had found love, thought of it as a "feeling in my stomach. It's like a flock of butterflies fluttering around." Unfortunately, she had confused love with indigestion.

But what is love? We use the word so loosely. We love ice cream and racquetball and a good movie. We also love the Church and the ways of the Lord. Certainly, we love our mates and our children and our God—yet we don't mean the same thing in relation to each object of our affections.

Have we, like Humpty Dumpty, decided this word can mean anything we choose it to mean? Did the Lord do so good a job of confusing our speech at Babel that we can no longer understand ourselves, much less each other?

Earlier, we made the point that we are not given the authority to define "love" any way we please. When we are commanded to love each other, we are also told what kind of love we should show. In John 13, love's definition is tied to the example of Jesus. But the Bible defines "love" not only with examples but also by careful word choice.

THE FOUR LOVES

While the English language relies heavily on the one word *love* to express a vast array of meanings, Greek, the language of the New Testament, used at least four different words to distinguish different kinds of love.

Eros

The first Greek word for love is a word having to do primarily with self. *Eros* is self-satisfying love. It can describe our love for food or water. It can also describe sensual pleasures or our sexual appetites. In fact, the strong connection between this word and sensuality is reflected by the meaning of our English adjective "erotic."

Although *eros* is self-satisfying and tends toward selfishness, it is not inherently evil. *Eros* is essential at times. Our desire for food or water or the opposite sex is God-given and right—in context. But uncontrolled, *eros* can enslave and allow selfish desires to dominate a person's life. Trying to satisfy our need for love solely with *eros* can only leave us hollow, empty, and unfulfilled.

Storge

Another Greek word translated as "love" is *storge*—what we might call "family love." Someone has described it as "the emotional magnet that draws blood relatives together." According to the Greeks, there is some truth in the statement "Blood is thicker than water."

James grew up in a family of nine boys and one girl. "We fussed and fought with the best of them," he says. "And while we happily beat up on each other, no one else was allowed to do that. If the school bully picked on one of us, he had all ten of us to contend with."

That's the way it is with *storge*. Though we may disagree, a sense of family still binds us together. Whatever differences we may have, shared blood cements us as a family.

The concept of family love gets us together and keeps us together. *Storge* holds better than Elmer's glue and lasts much longer. It loses its strength only when stressed beyond all reasonable bounds.

Philia

The third word used in the Greek language for "love" is *philia*. Two English words derive from *philia*: philanthropy (love of humankind); Philadelphia (city of brotherly love).

The English word *like* is similar to this Greek word. When we speak of *philia,* we are actually talking about warm feelings of affection much akin to friendship. *Philia* is a natural affection felt for another human being. It is based on common interests and shared activity. In fact, the more interests you have in common, the more *philia* you have.

When a friend of ours married, his new wife asked if he wanted her to do things *for* him or *with* him. Being young and naive, he answered that he wanted her to do things with him.

"What do you like to do?" she asked. It so happened that he was an enthusiastic deer hunter. She balked at first, but then agreed to go along. Their shared activity created a real camaraderie and strengthened a *philia*-love. This worked great until she began to take more deer than he did!

But please notice: something can happen to this kind of love. If your walking partner decides she wants to stay home, or your fishing buddy decides he'd rather buy his fish from the supermarket, what happens to *philia*-love?

Philia lives or dies with the ups and downs of shared interests and activities. The key ingredient in *philia*-love is *response.* As long as there is response, there will be friendship. When response dies, the feeling suffers soon after.

Perhaps this is what ails many marriages. Marriages built primarily on *philia* demand constant infusion of shared interests. Husbands and wives in such relationships lose "that ol' feeling" when in time they stop sharing the pursuits which brought them together in the first place.

Failure to understand the limits of *philia*-love has led to many heartaches in marriages, in friendships, and in the Church. If we think of *philia* as the foundation for relationships, we set ourselves up for failure. So long as we get the right response, we feel the warm fuzzies we identify as love.

But when the response dies, *philia* dies, and we find ourselves longing for a more permanent base on which to found our relationships.

There must be a higher kind of love among Christians than any we have studied so far, a love to cement us together when *eros, storge,* and *philia* don't apply. Not every relationship can be built on self-gratification or blood relationship or shared interests. In fact, any relationship in the Church built primarily on these kinds of love is doomed to failure. There has to be a better way.

Agape

The fourth and most characteristically Christian kind of love is represented by the Greek word *agape.* Most of us have heard of *agape*-love. It delineates a love at the heart of the biblical message.

When we read phrases like "For God so loved the world that He gave His only begotten Son" (John 3:16), we are reading about *agape*-love. Paul says God loved us even while we were sinners (Romans 5:8). Again, he is speaking of this higher kind of love—*agape.* When Christ admonishes us to love our enemies, He uses the word *agape.*

Agape is unique among the other loves we have mentioned. It is based not on self-satisfaction or kinship or common interests—it is, rather, *the unconditional commitment to treat others as God has treated us. Agape* does not select whom it will love or how it will treat people on the basis of *their* qualities or attributes. When we possess *agape*-love, we treat others in a Christlike manner because of who *we* are, not who *they* are. We who have experienced the *agape*-love of God love others simply because we ourselves have been so richly loved.

In the Church are many who are unable or unwilling to "meet our needs." Can we love them even without an *eros* motive? Most of the people in the Church are not related to us by blood. Can we learn to experience a familial bond with these people in the absence of blood ties? Some in the local church will never share your love for knitting or horses or reading or singing—how can you love those with whom you have so little in common?

The answer is *agape*! The *agape*-lover treats people right *in spite* of who they are, not *because* of it. They may be of a different race, socio-economic status, or political leaning. They may have strange ideas or habits or lifestyles. They may even consider themselves our enemies. None of that matters. The *agape*-lover treats people right, remembering always that there was a time (not entirely passed) when he was well-loved in spite of not being well-behaved.

This *agape*-love is the thermostat controlling the environment in the local church. Each of the loves we have discussed has its proper role in the Body of Christ. There is room in the Church for *storge, philia,* even *eros.* But each of these can cause trouble in the Church unless there is a healthy dose of *agape. Eros* will look at people selfishly, primarily for the benefit they can yield. *Philia* will care only about people we feel naturally attracted to because of shared interests and gratifying responses. *Storge* will limit our interaction to blood relatives.

But *agape*-love constantly regulates our natural responses to people by tempering the human with the divine. Like a thermostat, *agape* keeps the Church's atmosphere at just the right temperature where godly relationships can flourish.

When people walk through the door of our church building, we don't have to decide whether to love them. That decision is already made! We don't need to know what he can do for us, whether she is a distant cousin, or what kinds of activities they enjoy. We have already made our decision because God has already loved *us* and is creating a new heart within us.

During the late 1960s, when college campuses burned with student unrest and the generation gap was alive and growing, a preacher in St. Louis introduced a college student to Jesus Christ. The long-haired, jean-clad young man was a gifted music major at Washington University.

It so happened that on the first Sunday morning this new Christian went to church, an old man led the singing. His voice cracked, he did not know how to beat time, and he didn't even sing in tune.

After worship, the young man rushed to the preacher and demanded, "Why would you let that old codger lead singing? He knows nothing about music and ruined the whole service! He was awful!"

The preacher said, "Do you remember our study of the love of God and how He accepts us in spite of what we are? That's how we are to love each other. That old man is your brother even though he may not be much of a song leader. You have to love him whether you like his singing or not."

The young man scratched his head, frowned, and walked in the direction of the old man. They stood before each other, a grey-haired retiree and a long-haired student. The young man wrapped the song leader in a huge bear hug and said, "You are the worst singer I've every heard, but I love you anyway!"

No wonder we call the Church a "relationship place." When *agape* reigns, people flourish, and the Church becomes what God intended it to be.

What is love? As we have seen, it seems like all things to all people. But in the Church, love is first and foremost a decision to treat people as God has treated us. We are not free to make of Christian love anything we wish. Jesus, through His example and by His teaching, calls us to a

higher form of loving in His Church, the love exemplified in
that beautiful thirteenth chapter of 1 Corinthians:

> Love is patient, love is kind. It does not envy, it does
> not boast, it is not proud. It is not rude, it is not self-
> seeking, it is not easily angered, it keeps no record of
> wrongs. Love does not delight in evil but rejoices with
> the truth. It always protects, always trusts, always
> hopes, always perseveres. Love never fails. (1 Corin-
> thians 13:4-8)

THE ONE WAY

Though there may be four ways to categorize love, there is
only one way to put it into practice. We can meditate about
love all day, and not change much about the way we deal
with our brothers and sisters. How, then, does *agape*-love
become real in our lives?

Most people think of love primarily as an emotion.
When we see love as a feeling, we find ourselves in a
quandary when the commandment to love confronts us.
How can God command us to *feel* a certain way? Does He
expect us to be so in control of our emotions that we can
summon warm and fuzzy feelings on demand? If it is necessary to *feel* loving toward people before we can claim to be
obedient to God's statute, each of us is in trouble.

Surprisingly, *agape* does not belong primarily to the
realm of the heart. It has most to do with behavior. *Agape* is
not a matter of what you feel for others so much as how you
behave toward them. If Christlike love and godly relationships are ever to become a reality in your life, you must
decide to *act*. Enough of trying to *emote* your way to better
relationships. Be done with attempting to *feel* your way into
action. There is only one way to *agape*-love: Start acting

toward others as Jesus has acted toward you.

Isn't it hypocrisy to act lovingly when we don't feel loving? If we think love is a sentiment of the heart, then anything that does not spring from tender emotions *is* a sham. The feelings must come first, then the actions.

Agape insists that the opposite is true. Behaving in loving ways despite the absence of loving feelings is not hypocrisy. It is the most beautiful form of obedience. Far from proving our insincerity, such behavior shows our determination to obey first and feel second. Christ wasn't demanding tender feelings when He told us to love our enemies. He didn't ask Peter to gush with emotion when he forgave his brother "seventy-seven times." And Christ certainly wasn't keen on the idea of a cross when He determined to drink the cup His Father had prepared for Him. Emotion is not the issue with *agape*-love. Obedience is.

Agape-love promises that when we act in love toward each other, feelings eventually will follow. What may begin as an action born of sheer discipline will eventually result in a nature which responds easily with compassion and love. Jesus doesn't call this process hypocrisy. He calls it growth.

A number of years ago, an elder of his church taught James how to play golf. (James still hasn't forgiven him.) James figured golf would be an easy game. All he had to do was hit a silly little ball—and he'd been playing baseball all his life! So he chose a golf club, put a ball on the tee, and grabbed that club like it was a baseball bat.

His friend just laughed and said, "You'll never hit it that way!"

"Just watch me!" James boasted, and began to flail away. After about the third try, he connected and dribbled the ball into the rough a few feet away.

With a barely suppressed guffaw, the friend proceeded to show James the correct manner in which to strike a golf ball. He explained stance and shoulder rotation and the interlocking grip. When he had James thoroughly tied in knots, he said, "*Now* hit the ball."

"I thought he had gone bananas," James says. "It didn't feel right. I felt uncomfortable and awkward and unnatural. I much preferred my baseball grip to this exercise in contortion. I did consent (in deference to my friend) to practice this new stroke a few hundred times."

James has played golf for some years now. Guess how he holds a golf club today? What began as contortion is now the only golf swing that feels comfortable. What once seemed so awkward is now the most natural thing in the world.

So it is with love. If we begin to *act* in *agape*-love toward others in our congregations—irrespective of our emotions or the awkwardness we may feel—soon we find the action has changed our feelings.

Do you think a particular brother is a bit strange? Show him a little *agape*. Your disapproval will soon dissolve into acceptance. Do you react with irritation to a sister? Show her a little *agape*. Your anger may well grow into patience. Are you exchanging hot words and cold stares with some in your congregation? Show them a little *agape*. You'll be surprised how quickly your behavior can change your emotions.

THE CHOICE

If you want to build your life on *eros*, the world is waiting for you to join forces with it. If you want to build your life on *storge*, locking your heart to all who do not share your blood, there are plenty in the world who have done just that. And if you want to build your life on *philia*, simply find people as much like yourself as possible to shower your

affections upon. That is the kind of love the world understands best of all.

The real difference between the people of the world
and the people of Christ is that we have determined to build
our lives on *agape*. We have determined to treat other
people like God has treated us.

It takes courage. Courage to act better than you feel.
Courage to give better than you get. But we've seen that
courage before. It's Cross-courage, Gethsemane-grit. Because Jesus built His life on *agape*, we who were nothing are
now sons and daughters of God. People all around you wait
for a similar love to transform their lives in a similar way.

DISCUSSION, REFLECTION, AND ACTION

Chapter Discussion

1. a. Go around the room and let each person describe a
time when he or she has experienced *eros* for a person,
food, or some other pleasure.
   b. Now do the same for *storge, philia,* and *agape*.

2. Divide the group into subgroups of two people each. Pair
up with someone you don't live with. Take five minutes to
make a list of the differences between the two of you and
another list of the similarities.

3. a. Now regather as a whole group. How do you feel when
the differences between you and another person are
pointed out?
   b. What kind of love do you think keeps this group
together, and why?

4. a. In question 1 you described times when you experi-

enced *agape* for someone, when you showed unconditional love for him or her. How did loving someone
like this make you feel?

b. What response did you receive from the other person?

5. Ask someone from your group to give an example from
his or her own life where *philia* is not working. Let the group
wrestle with possible reasons why it is not working and then
see if *agape* might suggest solutions.

Personal Bible Search

1. Read 1 Corinthians 13:4-8.
   a. List the characteristics of love named in this passage.
   b. Compare the way different Bible translations render
   these various characteristics.
   c. Take a few minutes and reorder the list from the most
   difficult to the least difficult for you personally.

2. Read Galatians 5:22-26.
   a. Can you think of someone who has all the characteristics of the fruit of the Spirit? If you can, how do you
   think he or she attained them?
   b. What does Paul mean by "living by the Spirit"?
   c. What is the opposite of living by the Spirit? Describe it
   in your own words. Consider your own experience.
   d. Do the characteristics of the fruit of the Spirit just come
   to us, or must we cultivate them? Why?

3. Read 1 Thessalonians 3:11-13.
   a. Should your daily prayer be that God might increase
   your love? Why or why not?
   b. If you believe it should be, will you commit yourself to
   pray daily for the next week that your love may increase
   more and more?

c. From where does the strength come to live a life of *agape*?

Personal Reflection and Action

1. Try to think of a time in Jesus' life when He exhibited each of the characteristics of love listed in 1 Corinthians 13. You might go through one of the gospels to find examples.

2. Should a person feel his way into actions or act his way into feelings? Why do you think so?

3. Psalm 119:11 says, "Your word have I hidden in my heart that I might not sin against you." Write out a scripture about love, such as John 13:34-35 or 1 Corinthians 13:4-8. Place it where you will see it several times each day. Read it aloud six times each day until you have memorized it. Then recite it once each day.

4. What are the three relationships that you value most? What kinds of love are these the results of?

CHAPTER SIX

A Declaration of Dependence

Some 300 years ago, John Donne penned the following words in *Holy Sonnets*:

> No man is an *Iland,* intire of it selfe; every man is a peece of the *Continent,* a part of the *maine*; if a *Clod* bee washed away by the *Sea, Europe* is the lesse. . . . Any mans death diminishes *me,* because I am involved in *Mankinde*; And therefore never send to know for whom the *bell* tolls; It tolls for *thee.*

Donne's words accurately reflect something about the rural mindset of the past. People once were connected to each other in a way that is almost incomprehensible to modern men and women. The slave of ancient Greece, the serf in medieval France, the farmer in Renaissance Italy was born, raised, married, and buried on the same few acres of land. His occupation was monotonously stable. His father's house, in time, became his house and, in turn, was passed on to his children. Families were extended, neighbors were permanent, and friendships could be lifelong.

That sense of permanence impacted how people of the past viewed reality, their commitments to others, and even

79

themselves. There once was a time when men and women defined themselves primarily in terms of *groups*. They identified themselves by clan or guild or social class. They thought in group terms and made decisions based on group standards. In the past, individuals were so tied to other people that they unconsciously evaluated every action in light of its effect on people surrounding them. In the nature of things, they were less individuals than "a part of the *maine*."

"OH THE TIMES, THEY ARE A-CHANGING."

If Donne spoke well for the masses of his own day, he increasingly fails to speak for today's modern industrialized city-dweller. In 1965 we found a new poet more to our liking. Paul Simon penned a hymn in praise of the individual, a man not only independent of others but fiercely proud of his freedom from the group. "I am a rock, I am an island," wrote Simon, and in a phrase, he captured a crucial difference between the past and the present.[1]

While permanence was characteristic of days gone by, transience is the norm of life today. In every aspect of modern life stability has been exchanged for novelty. We love change. Where we live, what we do for a living, even who we count as friend and family are in constant flux. Alvin Toffler, author of *Future Shock*, wrote:

> In each year since 1948 one out of five Americans changed his address, picking up his children, some household effects, and starting life anew at a fresh place. Even the great migrations of history, the Mongol hordes, the westward movement of Europeans in the nineteenth century, seem puny by statistical comparison.[2]

Transience also extends to the way we work. "Under conditions prevailing at the beginning of the 1960's," states a report by the U.S. Department of Labor, "the average twenty-year-old man in the work force could be expected to change jobs about six or seven times." We no longer speak of choosing a single lifelong career; the salesperson of today could be the author of tomorrow and the professor of the day after.

Even relationships are not immune to the pressure of transience.

> Our friends float past; we become involved with them; they float on, and we must rely on hearsay or lose track of them completely; they float back again, and we must either renew our friendship—catch up to date—or find that they and we don't comprehend each other any more.[3]

The vast distances separating many extended families and the rising rate of divorce ensure that our familial relationships display the same characteristics. Even immediate family members are becoming strangers for many in our society.

This sense of transience impacts how we view reality, our commitments to people, and even ourselves. We no longer define ourselves in corporate terms. We don't make decisions primarily on the basis of how other people would be affected or what would be beneficial for the group. We belong to the "me" generation; we have entered the Age of Individualism. We have become a people who unconsciously evaluates every action primarily in terms of how it affects self. The people of the present no longer see themselves as a "part of the maine." They are rocks. They are islands.

INDIVIDUALISM AND THE CHURCH

An essential challenge of the Church today is to teach the individualist how to act as "a peece of the *Continent,* a part of the *maine.*" Put simply, the Church is faced with teaching the "me" generation how to think in "we" terms. People born and reared in a culture that worships individualism must now learn how to behave in a group—the Church. A new set of attitudes and skills is demanded if the individual is to live as a part of the body.

It is fair to say that most people entering the Church today are simply not equipped to think in group terms. Dependency, we have learned, is weakness; accountability is slavery; submission is demeaning. The very notion of denying self to promote the group is alien to the modern mind. To say that the unity of the Church may be more important than individual interests and freedoms is tantamount to cultural heresy.

Unfortunately, the contemporary church has not come to grips with this reality. While we require new members to learn some basic theology and to conform to a basic code of ethics, rarely do we teach them how to "conduct themselves in God's household, which is the church of the living God" (1 Timothy 3:15). Rarely do we train them in group attitudes and skills necessary to harmoniously function in the Body of Christ. We seem to assume converts being incorporated into the Church already know how to think and behave in corporate terms.

Nothing could be further from the truth. Most church members are individualists in Sunday-go-to-meeting clothing. They still think in "me" terms. They make decisions and act not based on what is good for the group, but on personal preferences and values. In the mind of most modern Christians, the needs of the many often take a back seat to the needs of the few or even the one.

None of this is to say that the problem of self-centeredness as opposed to group-centeredness is unique to our time, only that it is more pronounced. Christianity has always struggled to teach its adherents the necessity of dying to self and behaving in a manner that builds up the body. Even the first century Church had its share of individualists.

It is interesting to note that the early Church was primarily a Church of the city, its character and difficulties shaped by an urban environment. Some of the same factors that make each of us an island were at work in the cities where Christianity first took root. In many ways, early Christians had more in common with the men and women of the present than with their own first-century rural contemporaries.

It is not surprising, then, to find Paul fighting just the kind of individualistic thinking that plagues the Church today. Those early urban Christians struggled as we do with learning to live corporately, to act for the good of the whole, and to value the needs of the many over the needs of the few. Paul had to address this problem among Christians at Rome, Corinth, Ephesus, and Philippi. Many of them, like many of us, did not know how to live in the kind of community Christ envisioned when He established His Church. While Paul's writings on this point were aimed at an audience 2000 years removed, the lessons he taught are tailor-made for the Church today.

TROUBLE IN PHILIPPI

Take the Philippian congregation as an example. Philippi was a small but cosmopolitan city, rich in history by the time Paul preached in its streets and markets. As one of the way-stations along the *Via Egnatia* (the major overland route connecting Rome with the markets of the East), Philippi hosted a wide variety of traders and travelers. It was here that Antony and Octavian conquered the armies of Brutus and Cassius (the assassins of Julius Caesar). In time, Octavian fortified Philippi and established a military outpost. When Paul came to this city, its inhabitants were mainly Roman, although Greeks and Jews were represented. In every way, Philippi provided just the environment Paul sought for preaching the gospel—a diverse, bustling metropolis set at a crossroad of trade and political life.

That environment, however, breeds the individualism that always threatens unity in a local church. In Philippi, for instance, slavery and international trade as well as the demands of Roman military life dislocated whole segments of the population from their countries and families. (When people are disconnected from their roots, they grow more likely to act from self-interest.) There was a diverse assortment of cultures, philosophies, and religions in the Roman, Greek, and Jewish segments of Philippian society. (Variety may be the spice of life, but it is also an acid that eats at the bonds of community. When the melting pot breaks down shared mores and customs, people feel less responsibility to society than to themselves.) While the urban environment of Philippi had commercial and political advantages, the sheer size and transience of its population (as in all urban centers) made communal living a less desirable option than the single-minded pursuit of personal interests.

Almost ten years after founding the church in Philippi, Paul received word that serious problems had arisen. Two of the most dedicated women in the congregation were at odds with one another, and their bickering had caused unpleasant difficulties in the church (Philippians 4:2). Pride and selfish ambition had reared their ugly heads, and the precious unity of the body was at risk.

Paul wrote immediately to the Philippians, and although he did not mention the rift between Euodia and Syntyche until chapter 4, he taught throughout the letter some essential lessons on corporate living. The crux of his message came in 2:2-8, where Paul reminded his readers of some basic rules for being "a peece of the *Continent*":

> [Be] like-minded, having the same love, being one in spirit and purpose. Do nothing out of selfish ambition or vain conceit, but in humility consider others better than yourselves. Each of you should look not only to your own interests, but also to the interests of others. Your attitude should be the same as that of Christ Jesus:
> > Who, being in very nature God,
> > > did not consider equality with God
> > > > something to be grasped,
> > but made himself nothing,
> > > taking the very nature of a servant,
> > > being made in human likeness.
> > And being found in appearance as a man,
> > > he humbled himself
> > > and became obedient to death—
> > > > even death on a cross!

As we will see, Paul aimed in this passage to deliver a mortal blow to individualistic thinking within the church. He asked his readers to rediscover a sense of connectedness and to immerse themselves in the life of the group. Unity, not self-actualization, is the goal of congregational life. It is the *body's* good, not an individual's fulfillment which must motivate each member's thoughts and actions. As members of a body, Christians must learn to subordinate themselves for the benefit of the congregation. Only then can the tyranny of the "I" yield to the fellowship of the "WE."

RULE #1: BE ONE

Philippians 2:2 provides the melody for this magnificent hymn on Church life: "Think alike. Love alike. Be of one soul. Be of one mind."[4]

Four times in this single verse, Paul stresses the importance of thinking in group terms. We who were many are now one. We who were so different are now alike. We revel in our oneness with others. Knowing only too well what it means to be an island, we prize our new-found unity in the Body of Christ.

Paul teaches that as a member of the Church my thoughts, my emotions, my very soul and mind are incorporated into the personality of the congregation. The goal of each Christian is to be one with the rest—to share the same mind, heart and soul with brothers and sisters. While the individualist marches to his different drummer, the Christian concentrates on marching in step with his fellows.

Please understand that Paul is not arguing for cookie-cutter Christians. He is not saying that we should all hold identical opinions or strive for bland uniformity. Don't confuse "like-mindedness" with photocopy Christianity.

Paul *is* saying, however, that the Christian longs to be "in sync" with other Christians. A disciple wants to be moving in the same direction, working toward the same goals, sharing a common purpose and affection with the rest of the Church. Like a good marriage, a good fellowship depends on members who are more concerned about the union than they are about personal interests and self advancement. Wasn't that the idea Jesus had in mind when He prayed . . .

that all of them may be one, Father, just as you are in me and I am in you. May they also be in us so that the world may believe that you have sent me. I have given them the glory that you gave me, that they may be one as we are one: I in them and you in me. May they be brought to complete unity to let the world know that you sent me and have loved them even as you have loved me. (John 17:21-23)

The late Ira North was asked how the great Madison, Tennessee, church numbering more than 3000 members had avoided any serious splits in its long history. He replied, "We talk about unity on Sunday morning and again on Sunday night and then again on Monday, Tuesday, Wednesday, Thursday, Friday, and Saturday. Then we start all over talking about it the next Sunday."

If the local church is ever to become the relationship place God intended, members must first value oneness of mind, heart, soul, and purpose. They must desire to make Jesus' prayer a reality in their local congregation. Unity must become for each Christian a treasured possession worth talking about and working for.

How is this kind of oneness possible? How can individual Christians make such unity a reality? Paul deals next with practical attitudes and skills that foster this group identity.

RULE #2: BE HUMBLE

Do nothing out of selfish ambition or vain conceit, but in humility consider others better than yourselves.
(Philippians 2:3)

Again, Paul strikes at the "me" orientation prevalent in our culture. In a society that buys millions of copies of a magazine called *Self* it is dangerous to insist that nothing should be done "out of selfish ambition." And in a society that made *Looking Out for Number One* a runaway best seller it is almost blasphemous to command that we should consider others better than ourselves.

But if the Church is serious about unity, it must take to heart Paul's comments on humility. Oneness in the local church remains an impossible dream as long as selfish ambition and conceit characterize her members. At the core of both vices is the individualism that destroys unity because it cares little for the *body's* well-being: self must be advanced at all cost, ego must be stroked at others' expense.

Instead, Paul advocates a radical humility—one which goes so far as to count others better than self, embracing a group attitude that counteracts any individualistic ambition and pride. This humility is not self-depreciation or a lack of healthy confidence, nor does considering others better mean overestimating their abilities or failing to see their faults.

What Paul proposes is, rather, a conscious decision to sit at the foot of the table so that others may be honored. It makes no difference that they may be new Christians while we are veterans. It doesn't matter that they struggle with sins we have long since conquered. It isn't even important that they desire the best seat because of their own selfish ambition and vain conceit. For the benefit of the body and in defense of unity, we grant respect "for each other, not on this ground or that, perhaps *without* any grounds, *counter* to every ground, simply because we are bidden" to do so.[5]

In the fall of 1921, a group of Christians met in Nashville, Tennessee, to plan a city-wide gospel meeting. They decided to rent the old Ryman Auditorium (made famous as the first home of the Grand Ole Opry) and ask the best speaker they could find to preach the meeting. It would take a special preacher to fill the 8000-seat auditorium for each night of the meeting.

The choice of speaker was finally narrowed down to two men: C.M. Pullias and N.B. Hardeman. Both were respected evangelists well-known in the Nashville area. Each man was contacted about this opportunity and asked to check his calendar. Both were available for the meeting.

After much discussion, the committee decided to ask Hardeman to preach and Pullias to conduct the singing. They were nervous, however, about asking Pullias to take the less prestigious role and wondered how he might react.

Pullias's response is a model of Christian humility. He graciously consented to lead the singing with these words: "I will gladly sweep the floors of Ryman Auditorium so that the gospel of Christ can be preached." On March 28, 1922, every seat of that auditorium was filled and more than 2000 people had to be turned away.

That kind of humility is incredibly difficult. Fortunately, it is the attitude Jesus portrayed. Because He came not to be served but to serve, and because He respected us above Himself—*without* any grounds, *counter* to every ground—we have been given the power to become better people. Perhaps the same grace will be extended to our brothers and sisters if a few of us can muster that kind of humility.

RULE #3: BE CONCERNED

Each of you should look not only to your own interests, but also to the interests of others.

(Philippians 2:4)

One of the prime symptoms of a "me" mindset is tunnel vision—a narrow and exclusive focus on personal agendas, hobbies, and interests. My programs must be advanced, my priorities must take precedence, my perspectives are most valid. Individualism at its worst is the failure to recognize that others may have interests that, though different from our own, are equally legitimate.

A "we" mindset yields an entirely different attitude. Because we are striving to be group-centered, our brothers' and sisters' priorities become our priorities. We are as concerned to see others' interests advanced as we are to see our own affairs prosper. Suddenly, what other Christians see as important becomes important to us as well.

Again, Jesus exemplified this kind of thinking throughout His lifetime. Whether it was pausing in His teaching long enough to heal a paralytic or granting forgiveness to a thief at the moment He was dying for the sins of the world, Jesus was never so wrapped up in His own agenda that He couldn't make time for others. Their concerns were always His concerns. It didn't matter that His priorities were spiritual and theirs physical, His eternal and theirs temporal, His earth-shattering and theirs mundane. Jesus always looked to the interests of others even as He focused on the task God had given Him to accomplish.

In that same spirit, Christians are no longer free to blindly pursue personal causes. The agenda of each Christian must be lengthened to include the agenda of every Christian. We are one in spirit and purpose. We consider one another better than ourselves. As a result, we pay close attention to the things which interest each other and do all in our power to seek one another's good.

SUMMARY: HAVE THIS MIND AMONG YOU

Paul concludes his lesson on community living by pointing us to the example of Jesus Christ. There is no greater argument against the individualistic lifestyle than the life of Jesus. While many Christians are still looking out for number one, Jesus lived looking out for *everyone*. Certainly, He was "the Rock"—but He was surely no island. Throughout Scripture, Jesus shows Himself to be the consummate "we" thinker.

As we have already seen, the life of Christ exemplifies each of the rules Paul gives for living in the body. But Paul, not wanting the Philippians to miss the point, insists that group-centeredness (as opposed to self-centeredness) is precisely what Jesus was all about.

Through Philippians 2:5-8 we see God who became so *one* with us that He was "found in appearance as a man." Here is a Man so *humble* that He "made himself nothing, taking the very nature of a servant." Here is a Servant so *concerned* about our interests that He "became obedient to death—even death on a cross."

Had Jesus bought into the attitudes of the "me" generation, He would have clung to His preeminence at any cost. Had He been an individualist, He would never have emptied Himself and taken on the nature of a servant. Had Jesus been looking out for Himself, He would not have gone to the cross.

Had Jesus shared the mindset of many in the Church today, we can be sure that He would have put His needs before ours, His good above ours, His interests ahead of ours. Fortunately, it is the disciple's task to imitate his Master, not vice versa. When we are like Christ, laying down our lives and taking up our crosses, we make unity in the body a real possibility.

His is the attitude Christians must imitate. It is time for us to throw off the shackles of self-centeredness. For too long, Christians have crippled the Church by their inability to think beyond themselves. If the Church is ever to be a body—a living, breathing, vital organism—members must recognize that the needs of the many outweigh the needs of the few. The tyranny of the individual must yield to the unity of the whole.

So be one who thinks of others—do everything in your power to keep in step with your brothers. Be humble—put the wants and needs of others ahead of your own. Be concerned—learn to appreciate and value the priorities of other Christians.

Above all, be Christlike. Pour yourself out. Become a servant. Lay down your life. When this is accomplished, there will be no more individualists in God's body. Instead our motto will be, "All for one and one for all." Easy? No! But if the three musketeers could do it, a few committed Christians should be equal to the task.

DISCUSSION, REFLECTION, AND ACTION

Chapter Discussion
1. a. Take a minute and write down the names of the first five people who pop into your mind. Do this as a brainstorming session by yourself.
   b. Now go around the group and have each person give one name and explain why it appears on the list.

2. Go around the room and answer these two questions:
   • Today, do you live more like an island or like a piece of a continent?
   • Five years ago, were you more like an island than you are now, or less?

3. According to the authors, what are some cultural factors that make it hard for Christians not to live as islands?

4. The JOY principle is: J—Jesus first.

O—Others second.

Y—Yourself last.

Do you think the JOY principle is biblical? Why or why not?

Personal Bible Search

1. Read Acts 4:32-36.
   a. How are the early believers described?
   b. What was the evidence of their unity?
   c. What attitudes did these believers show toward each other? How do you think they attained these attitudes?

2. Read Acts 5:1-11.
   a. Compare the attitudes of Barnabas (Acts 4:36-37) and Ananias. What differences do you observe?
   b. What is the proper use of the things God gives us?

3. Read James 3:13-18.
   a. Describe the attitude toward the Body of Christ that a person who harbors envy and selfish ambition has.
   b. What is the result of such attitudes?
   c. What are the characteristics of heavenly wisdom? Explain what James says in your own words.

Personal Reflection and Action

1. How do personal agendas sometimes hinder local unity?

2. Is it reasonable to assume that our attitude could be like Christ's (Philippians 2:5)? Why or why not?

3. Look up *kenosis* in a good dictionary. Write out the definition. Does your dictionary list a biblical reference? What does this reference tell you about how Christians should act?

CHAPTER SEVEN

Of Peacocks, Cranes, and Christians

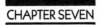

About 600 years before Christ, a Greek slave named Aesop developed a reputation for wisdom. His stories of birds and beasts—with the inevitable moral at the end of each tale—have continued through the centuries to educate men and women about themselves. In one fable, Aesop uses a peacock and a crane to teach a lesson much needed by the Church today.

> The Peacock and the Crane happened to meet one day and the Peacock spread his beautiful tail, and minced around and looked with contempt at the Crane as though it were just an ordinary creature and not worthy of his proud notice.
>
> The Crane didn't like this insolent, haughty behavior, so he said, just loudly enough for the Peacock to hear him, "Peacocks would be fine birds if fine feathers could make them so, but it must be terrible not to be noble enough to fly up above the clouds." Then the Crane flapped his large, strong wings and sailed away, leaving the Peacock below not half so pleased with himself as he had been before.
>
> *The Point*—It is foolish to insult others

because they are not like us. In many ways they may
be much better than we are.[1]

LESSONS FROM A PEACOCK AND A CRANE

A rabid individualism threatens the unity of congregations
throughout our country. While the "me" generation pursues
its agenda of self-interest, the body life of the Church atro-
phies into impotence. We are convinced that Christians
must learn to be group-centered, or else there is little hope
of making the Church a true fellowship.

Having made that point as strongly as we know how, it
is now our task to argue that Christians face another—and
paradoxical—challenge. In our eagerness to promote oneness of the body, we must not be so zealous that we mistake
homogenization for harmony. Those of us who have
renounced individualism must at the same time learn to
value the diversity of individuals. Even as we strive for
oneness, it is vital that we allow others their little differences.

So long as the Church is made up of people, diversity will
be inescapable in our congregations. Ignore it if you want.
View it as a necessary evil if you must. Sing its praises or shout
its problems. Whatever you choose to do about diversity, it
won't go away. The Church today must learn to appreciate
diversity as one of the foremost strengths of God's people.

The same God who made the peacock and the crane
made Peter and Paul, John and Thomas. In the Church as in
the fable, it is foolish to condemn others because they are
unlike us. In many ways they may be much better.

UNITY AND DIVERSITY: A CASE STUDY

When the Apostle Paul stated that "there is no Greek or Jew,
circumcised or uncircumcised, barbarian, Scythian, slave or

free, but Christ is all, and is in all" (Colossians 3:11), he exaggerated slightly to make a point. There *were* Greeks and Jews, slaves and free, male and female, rich and poor in the churches of the first century. Just because these people had become Christians, they had not lost their cultural heritage or religious background or social status. Paul did not say there were no differences between members of the early Church, only that such differences need not threaten the unity of a group glued together by Jesus Christ. He was not arguing against diversity, but for unity in the midst of diversity.

The New Testament Church was about as diverse a group of people as you could imagine. Many Christians (like Matthew) were Jewish; many others (like Cornelius) were Gentiles; a few (like Timothy) were a mixture of both. Some (Apollos, for example) were well-educated and wealthy; others (Peter and John) were poor and unschooled. Some had grown up in a conservative religious background (like Paul); others (as in the Corinthian church) had grown up worshiping local gods with shrine prostitutes. Some were hotheaded and passionate (Peter); others were warm and loving (Barnabas); still others were cool and logical (Luke). Many (like Philemon) were free; many others (Onesimus, for instance) were slaves. Every congregation contained a cross-section of the community from which it was drawn. There was no such thing as a *typical* Christian; there was as much variation within the Church as without.

The bloodiest battle fought in the first-century Church centered on this issue of diversity. Should the Church eliminate all differences for the sake of oneness? Was unanimity necessary to attain functional unity? How do you make one Church out of so many different ingredients?

During the earliest days of the Church, Christians had a great deal in common with one another. They were all Jews.

They all shared the same heritage and tradition. They had been raised worshiping the same God, reading the same religious literature, and living by the same standards and moral codes. They dressed alike, honored the same days, avoided the same kinds of foods. They shared the same heroes, abhorred the same sins, prayed identical prayers. No wonder those first months of the Church in Jerusalem have served as a model of unity and togetherness ever since.

So long as Christianity remained a "Jewish" religion limited to Jerusalem and a few outlying pockets of Jewish culture, the Church could afford to maintain a unity based on its essential homogeneity. But God never intended Christianity to remain within the womb of Judaism. From the time of Abraham, God was determined to bless "all nations of the earth" (Genesis 12:3). The prophets foretold that the Gentiles would be included in the blessings of the Messiah. Jesus Himself came and insisted that there were other sheep "not of this sheep pen. I must bring them also. They too will listen to my voice, and there shall be one flock and one shepherd" (John 10:16).

Nothing could have threatened the unity of the Church more, however, than attempting to include this group of people so completely different from the Jews. Jews had intense contempt for Gentiles. They called Gentiles "dogs" and "uncircumcised," believing that the only reason God had created the "nations" was as fuel for the fires of hell. To the Jews, Gentiles were immoral and unspiritual. They had no religion except for the paganism and polytheism the Jews so disdained. They ate unclean foods and lived unclean lifestyles. Gentiles even smelled unclean.

What a shock it must have been, then, when no less a stickler for Jewish ways than Peter ushered Cornelius into the Church. Immediately the believers criticized Peter for including an outsider and Peter found himself in Jerusalem defending his actions. To the credit of the Jerusalem leadership, they quickly accepted that "even the Gentiles" were to be included within the scope of the gospel (Acts 11:18).

Having allowed Gentiles into the Church, however, some launched a concerted effort to make the Gentiles as Jewish as possible, requiring them to be circumcised and obey the law of Moses (Acts 15:5). To a certain element of Jewish Christians, only remaking the Gentile converts along Jewish lines could maintain the Church's unity. Gentile Christians had to bear the covenant mark (circumcision), observe the covenant laws, and presumably even honor the broader customs and traditions of the covenant people. They had to become as Jewish as the Jews in order to enjoy fellowship in the Church. Some ex-Pharisees, like some of us, could not understand that there was room in Christ's Body for diversity on such matters.

But the fact is that room has always existed in God's Church for diversity on a wide range of issues. Gentiles, with all their differences in background and behavior, were just as welcome in Christ's Church as Jews. You didn't have to be kosher to be Christian. Pork-eaters could rub shoulders with pork-haters. Synagogue attendance was not required, nor a pilgrimage to Jerusalem, nor the wearing of phylacteries and skull caps. Never was homogenization of the Church seen as an answer to the challenge of oneness.

ACCEPTANCE: THE KEY TO UNITY

The remarkable feature of the New Testament Church was not the similarity of its members, but its ability to maintain unity in diversity. How did they do it? How did first-century Christians manage to build a unified fellowship out of such a pluralistic membership?

The Apostle Paul did it by preaching acceptance rather

than conformity, love before law, respect instead of arbitrary standards. Far from suppressing variety, he gloried in it. The myriad faces of the Church only proved to Paul the universality of the gospel message and the power of the Christian bond. Where except under Christ's lordship could such diversity result in unity?

In his letter to the Romans, for instance, Paul stressed the need to accept individual differences within the Christian fellowship. Cloned Christians were not the goal of the Church. Rather, Paul aimed to develop an environment where diversity could be met with acceptance.

The particular issues causing concern for the Roman church seem minor and inconsequential to us. For them, however, the issues were serious. Sincere Christians disagreed over which foods to eat or which days to honor (see Romans 14-15).

> One man's faith allows him to eat everything, but
> another man, whose faith is weak, eats only vegeta-
> bles. . . . One man considers one day more sacred
> than another; another man considers every day alike.
> (Romans 14:2,5)

Underlying this conflict was probably an attempt by Jewish Christians to force conformity on their Gentile brethren. If the Jews could not bring themselves to eat certain foods, how could the Gentiles? Since some of these Jews continued to honor the Sabbath, surely the Gentiles should as well.

The church at Rome found its unity threatened by the diversity of its members. As is often the case, they concluded that this threat could be alleviated only by all members of the congregation acting alike. Those who refrained from eating certain foods began to pass judgment on those who indulged. Those able to eat freely in good conscience tried to ridicule their weaker brothers and sisters into more tolerant attitudes. Each side played the power game, the first group questioning the commitment of the second and the second group doubting the sanity of the first. Unless the eaters acknowledged the error of their ways, the non-eaters viewed them suspiciously. On the other hand, the eaters refused to allow their freedom to be impaired by the silly customs of their "weaker brothers," even when it caused those brothers to stumble.

Into this situation stepped the Apostle Paul, insisting that unity in the Body of Christ had nothing to do with uniformity on the part of its members. Sameness would not ensure oneness. Instead, Paul asked these Christians to accept diversity on disputable matters and to behave in such a way that the issues did not become divisive.

> Accept him whose faith is weak, without passing judgment on disputable matters. . . . The man who eats everything must not look down on him who does not, and the man who does not eat everything must not condemn the man who does, for God has accepted him.   (Romans 14:1,3)

It would have been easy enough for Paul to lay down one rule for all to follow, to support one side or the other in an effort to promote unity. But Paul saw a greater issue at stake here: keeping the body unified in the presence of diverse opinions. He knew that if it were not this issue it would be another over which brothers differed. The vital thing was to develop an attitude that promoted peace in the face of such diversity. Instead of laying down the law ("Everyone should eat" or "No one should eat"), Paul asked for *acceptance*—the realization that personal feelings about such matters should not be allowed to affect relationships.

Paul knew that some Christians had learned to enjoy their freedom in Christ. Not bound by past customs or religious traditions, they felt free to make choices on the basis of the mind of Jesus. Others in the Church, however, were not so strong in the faith. They continued to follow tradition from consciences still shaped by the thinking of their past. What was freedom for the one was sin for the other.

More important for Paul, however, was the way these two groups related to each other. For those whose consciences would not allow certain behaviors, the temptation was strong to condemn and judge those who saw things differently. For those who enjoyed a sense of freedom about such matters, the temptation was equally strong to ridicule and resent those who would limit their behavior.

For the Apostle, the critical issue was not determining who was right or wrong, but maintaining the unity of Christ's Body in the midst of these differences.

> Therefore let us stop passing judgment on one another. Instead, make up your mind not to put any stumbling block or obstacle in your brother's way. . . . For the kingdom of God is not a matter of eating and drinking, but of righteousness, *peace,* and joy in the Holy Spirit. . . . Let us therefore make every effort to do what leads to *peace* and to mutual edification.
> (Romans 14:13,17,19, emphasis added)

Paul argued that Christians must never let minor things interfere with the major. When differences on peripheral matters threaten the peace and joy of the Kingdom, believers have strained the gnat and swallowed the camel. Paul instead commanded his readers to aim at what is truly major: peace within the congregation.

For the Romans, that meant non-eaters must hold their tongues and refuse to pass judgment on brothers and sisters who think differently. Eaters, on the other hand, must not permit their freedom to become a stumbling block for more sensitive believers. The non-eater should allow others to do things his conscience would not allow for himself. The eater should abstain from things which his conscience allowed but which encouraged others to act against their consciences.

Paul's answer to diversity in the Church was not conformity but a spirit of acceptance and loving self-denial, which irresistibly leads to peace in the Church.

Paul gets to the core of his teaching by returning to a relationship rule we noticed in the last chapter:

> Each of us should please his neighbor for his good, to build him up. For even Christ did not please himself.
> (Romans 15:2-3)

Unity in the Church (then as now) depended on the willingness of her members to live for each other and "consider others better" than themselves (Philippians 2:3). The Romans were not a part of the body to advance their own causes or insist on their own ways. Rather, they were called to follow Christ's example, determining behavior by what is beneficial for others.

Paul concluded his teaching on diversity with a prayer that should be emblazoned on the walls of every church building and Christian home:

> May the God who gives endurance and encouragement give you a spirit of unity among yourselves as you follow Christ Jesus, so that with one heart and

mouth you may glorify the God and Father of our Lord Jesus Christ.

Accept one another, then, just as Christ accepted you, in order to bring praise to God. (Romans 15:5-7)

DIVERSITY IN THE CHURCH TODAY

Managing diversity is not just a first-century problem, for the same issues confront the Church today. Think about this. The Church in your community provides one of the few melting pots remaining in our culture. What organization or social group calls together the range of people found in the local church, where humans of every shape and description are thrown together and expected to form an intimate fellowship? From an incredible variety of people God promises to build one body.

Notice just a few of the differences people bring to our fellowships. We are varied as *people*. Black and white, rich and poor, young and old, white collar and blue collar, up-tight and laid-back. We have different cultures, values, appearances, and personalities. Some like rock and roll; others prefer Mozart. We are single and married and divorced. All of us have lived through the Great Depression; it's just that some of us refer to the crash of '29 while others mean what happened when they flunked chemistry. Within one group exist optimists and pessimists, thinkers and doers, hard-liners and soft-touches.

But that doesn't even scratch the surface. We also are varied as *Christians*. Some were raised in warm, vibrant, committed churches; some cut our religious teeth on legalism; some grew up in congregations more concerned with social status than with God's Word; and some of us never darkened the door of a church during our childhood. Side by side are Christians who have walked with the Lord for forty years and Christians who have walked with Jesus for four days. There are those who have grown to be spiritual giants and those who still need milk rather than meat. Some are liberals, some conservatives. Not a single individual in your congregation would agree with you on every issue facing the Church today. God gifted some of us to serve, some to teach, some to encourage, and others to lead (Romans 12:6-8). In this Body of Christ we find hands and feet, eyes and ears, tongues and toenails.

What then are we to do with all this diversity in the local church? Is it a strength or a weakness, a blessing or a curse? While we may like our milk homogenized, do we really prefer our churches that way?

If we are not careful, many members will continue to view diversity as a barrier to Christian oneness. Any plea for unity will degenerate into passion for uniformity. Unfortunately, there is a thin line between discouraging individualism and disparaging the individual.

But the oneness the New Testament extols has nothing to do with "standardized Christianity." The apostolic writers saw Church unity as rooted in something completely different from the pressure to conform to any standard other than Christ. To Paul, both the unity of the Body of Christ and the diversity of individual members were precious gifts of God to be protected and fought for. Unity is not an ideal for which individual Christians must suppress all differences, but a reality to which each individual uniquely contributes.

The lesson of the New Testament is clear. If unity is to flourish in the Church today, it will not be achieved through a pressure to conform. My own comfort zone cannot become the yardstick against which other Christians are measured. Whether weak or strong, we reach the heights of spiritual maturity only when we behave in a manner that builds up our brothers and sisters. Condemnation does not fall into that category, nor does ridicule. Only accepting legitimate differences qualifies us for a truly Christlike level of maturity.

As surely as Christians must struggle against the individualism of our time and culture, so too must we avoid the temptation to struggle against the individual. On our way to developing group-centeredness we must not forget to value the diversity of group members. Though Aesop said it first, Paul would echo the sentiment, "It is foolish to insult others because they are not like us. In many ways, they may be much better than we are."

There will never come a time in the Lord's Church when there is "no Greek or Jew, circumcised or uncircumcised, barbarian, Scythian, slave or free." So long as the Church draws breath, there will be differences in the people who gather to her. The challenge to the Church, then or now, is to appreciate that whatever our differences, "Christ is all, and is in all." With Christ in common, all other differences become insignificant.

Christ has accepted so much in each of us—so much that is inconsistent with His preferences, or immature by His standards, or incomplete according to His knowledge— that it smacks of ingratitude for us to be less accepting of our brothers and sisters. If Jesus can put up with the likes of us, we can manage at least grudging tolerance of each other!

DISCUSSION, REFLECTION, AND ACTION

Chapter Discussion

1. a. In what ways, if any, have you acted like a peacock recently?

   b. In what ways do you feel you have been treated recently the way the peacock treated the crane?

[*To the leader:* Does your group trust each other enough to answer question 1 candidly and lovingly?]

2. a. On page 99 the authors state, "Never was homogenization of the Church seen as an answer to the challenge of oneness." What do you think they mean by this statement?
   b. Do you agree or disagree? Explain your answer.

3. a. How did Paul deal with diversity in the Roman church?
   b. Which side in this controversy (the "eaters" or the "noneaters") do you think would have had the most difficulty accepting Paul's solution? Why?

4. How would you answer the question on diversity (page 105): "Is it a strength or a weakness, a blessing or a curse?" Why?

5. Discuss how this list of differences might affect your group:
   - optimists/pessimists
   - thinkers/doers
   - hardliners/soft-touches

6. Are there other differences within your group that need to be dealt with? If so, what do you need to do?

Personal Bible Search
1. Read Romans 12:3-8.
   a. Describe the way we ought to think of ourselves.
   b. What are the implications of the fact that each Christian belongs to one body?
   c. Investigate the meaning of each gift Paul lists. Then match the name of someone you know to each gift.

2. Read Romans 12:9-16.
   a. Make a list of the imperatives (commands, instructions) in these verses. Then ask yourself, "How am I doing at each of these?"
   b. Look up *proud* and *conceited* in a dictionary, and write the definitions that seem to fit these verses.

3. Read Romans 12:17-21.
   a. To what extent are we to live at peace with each other?
   b. What do you think this means in practical terms? Give an example from your own life.
   c. How do you suppose leaving revenge to God would help you get along better with others?
   d. What does it mean to "heap burning coals" on another person?

Personal Reflection and Action
1. Why do you think people have so much difficulty accepting differences in others?

2. This week as you go about your work, see if you can catch yourself before you are about to act negatively to a difference in another person. Ask God to enable you to substitute acceptance for judgment.

3. Think about how you would feel if suddenly everyone was exactly like you.

CHAPTER EIGHT

If This Is Peace, Who Needs War?

"I thought the Church was different." He looked wounded and confused and surprised. The bitter meeting the night before—some were dissatisfied with the work of our youth minister—had startled this young man. "I came to this church because I was looking for real relationships. I wanted to know how to treat people right. But what I saw last night convinced me that you don't know any more about that subject than I do!"

Ouch! What do you tell this young man? How do you answer the questions lurking beneath his disappointment and pain? Is there any difference between the Church and the world when it comes to conflict? Does a commitment to Jesus inoculate us against disagreement? Does such a commitment at least help us avoid the acrimony and venom that seem to go hand in hand with discord?

This young man is but a drop in the bucket. There are thousands like him in (and more often out of) our churches. When they see the ugliness of churches at war they wonder whether the call of Jesus Christ really teaches us how to treat people right. The answers we give to their questions in many ways determine the future of the Church. Most people are not looking for another boxing arena; they seek a haven of rest where they are not bruised and blood-ied every time differences arise.

A BRIEF HISTORY OF CHURCH CONFLICT

Jesus Himself insisted that He came not "to bring peace, but a sword" (Matthew 10:34). Surely, however, He did not intend His followers to take Him quite as literally as they have. Even a glance at the history of Christendom shows that those who claim to be Christ's disciples have behaved in some very unChristlike ways. Consider, for example, just one hundred years of Church history.

In AD 897, Pope Stephen VI had the corpse of Pope Formosa exhumed, dressed in purple robes, propped up before an ecclesiastical counsel and tried for certain doctrin-al errors. The corpse was found guilty, stripped, mutilated, and thrown into the River Tiber. Some time later, Stephen VI himself was strangled to death by another who desired the pontiff's chair.

Pope John X (AD 914-928) watched his brother die at the hands of an ambitious churchman attempting to force John from the papacy. About a year later, John was thrown into prison where he died of "unknown causes."

Benedict VI (973-974) was strangled by a Roman noble who made himself pope for a month and then absconded with all the papal treasure he could carry. Nine years later, this same nobleman returned, killed the reigning pope, and established himself as pope once more.

John XVI (997) was deposed. His eyes gouged out, his nose and tongue cut off, he was paraded through Rome's streets riding backward on a donkey.

Gregory V (999) died of poisoning.

Had enough? There's more. There were more than 200 years of Crusades, eight separate campaigns in which the so-called Christian nations set out to win the world for Jesus. The zealous Bernard of the Templars wrote:

> The Christian who slays the unbeliever in the holy war
> is sure of his reward; more sure if he himself is slain.
> The Christian glories in the death of the pagan,
> because Christ is thereby glorified.[1]

In many instances unbelievers were rounded up and given a simple choice: conversion or the sword. In Cologne (while the crusaders were on their way to the Holy Land and had some time on their hands), hundreds of Jews chose to kill themselves rather than submit to the Crusaders' ultimatum. Mothers giving birth to children during this time were said to have strangled their newborns rather than have them fall into the hands of Christians.

Had enough now? There's more. During the first half of this millennium (AD 1200-1500), the infamous Inquisition raged in Spain. The Roman church determined to stamp out the heresies that threatened her authority throughout Europe. Will Durant, in *A History of Civilization,* writes of this period:

> Compared with the persecution of heresy in Europe
> from 1227 to 1492, the persecution of Christians by
> Romans in the first three centuries after Christ was a
> mild and humane procedure. Making every allowance
> required of an historian and permitted to a Christian,
> we must rank the Inquisition . . . as among the darkest
> blots on the record of mankind, revealing a ferocity
> unknown in any beast.[2]

Had enough? Forgive us Father—there is more!
Lest you think all this is something we have put behind

us, something we have outgrown in more civilized times, remember that today in Ireland, Protestants long to kill Catholics and Catholics itch to kill Protestants. In Lebanon, Christians slay Moslems with as much glee as the Moslems who return the favor. (During the Middle East war of 1948, Warren Austin, then U.S. Ambassador to the United Nations, urged the Arabs and Jews to resolve their disagreements "like good Christians."[3] Not only did he show insensitivity to his audience, he forgot how "good Christians" have chosen to resolve their differences!)

Lest you think it is only in distant, more primitive lands where such atrocities exist, examine the present condition of the Church in America. Recent scandals among certain television ministries involving the grossest immoralities and financial improprieties have been outdone only by the war pulpit personalities have waged among themselves in a misguided attempt to straighten up each other's house. The entire world has looked on in awe and amused disgust as "Christians" have slandered, gossiped and reviled one another on television screens and front pages.

Certainly not everyone who wears the title "Christian" is a true disciple of our Lord. However, before we dismiss the above examples as abuses by people who are Christian in name only, there are two points we should keep in mind. First, the world is not always able to make a distinction between those who say "Lord, Lord," and those who do what the Lord commands (Luke 6:46). In the minds of many, the true disciple is guilty by association with those (past and present) who have claimed to act in the name of our Lord.

Second, those of us who believe ourselves to be Jesus' true representatives have enough dirty laundry to give most observers cause to wonder. Conflict is an all-too-personal experience for most Bible-believing Christians. Which of us has not witnessed a meeting of brothers and sisters degenerate into bitter finger-pointing and name-calling? We too know the agony of angry words and broken relationships. Few churches can claim a past unmarred by splits in the ranks. One of the ugliest statistics that can be leveled at the Church indicates that more congregations are started by disgruntled members who will no longer worship at a certain locale than by missionary members who plant churches to further the growth of the Kingdom.

It is true we refrain from murder and physical torture in Church conflicts today. But such restraint comes not from changed attitudes as much as from changed methods. We opt for more subtle techniques. While we don't stretch one another on physical racks, we feel no compunction about tying brothers to verbal racks and stretching them until they scream. While we may not kill with swords or guns, we manage nicely with editorial darts and deadly innuendo. In the end, the results are the same: assassinated characters and mortally wounded souls.

And all of this in the name of the Prince of Peace who came from the God of peace to preach a gospel of peace so we might "make every effort to do what leads to peace."

It makes us wonder if the prophets' words are more prophetic than we had imagined, applying as much to the Church today as to those to whom they were originally spoken:

> Their throats are open graves;
> their tongues practice deceit.
> The poison of vipers is on their lips.
> Their mouths are full of cursing and bitterness.
> Their feet are swift to shed blood;
> ruin and misery mark their ways,
> and the way of peace they do not know.
> (Romans 3:13-17)

A BRIEF HISTORY OF BIBLICAL CONFLICT

Given all the abuses of the past and present, it shouldn't surprise us to discover a growing belief among Christians that conflict has no place in the Church of Jesus Christ.

Nothing could be further from the truth. By its very nature the Christian community deals with matters of eternal importance, themes near to the hearts of both God and man. Whenever people deal with important issues there are bound to be conflicts of opinion. Moreover, even the most cursory reading of the New Testament demonstrates that the early Church itself was no stranger to dissension. Conflict is not simply a problem of the apostate Church; it was a reality in the apostolic Church as well. Simply because conflicts exist does not mean the Church has lost its way.

On numerous occasions the apostles argued with each other and even with Christ. Their conflicts did not even have the virtue of debating lofty ideals and themes. They argued out of selfish ambition. The picture of twelve grown men bickering over who would be the greatest in the Kingdom would be laughable were it not so sad and so much like ourselves. Peter even clashed with Jesus, once rebuking his Lord for speaking of the Cross, and on another occasion objecting to Jesus' washing feet. Yet such conflicts did not disqualify the apostles from their calling. They were apostles as much during their conflicts as before or after.

Christ Himself was not above a good tussle. With Peter, He gave as good as He got. His discussions with the Pharisees frequently erupted into verbal battles. Jesus' sharp wit and flawless logic often left His opponents' egos bruised and bloodied. He who made a whip in the Temple and spoke the woes of Matthew 23 was not one who shrank from conflict. Do we think any less of Jesus for His capacity to experience and express anger?

Just weeks after the Church was established, conflict arose in the ranks of the Jerusalem congregation. The sixth chapter of Acts reports murmuring among the Grecian element because their widows were being neglected in the daily distribution of food. Only by calling a church-wide assembly and handling the problem decisively did the apostles avoid an ethnic split in the church. Far from suppressing conflict, the apostles read it as a signal for change. Certainly they did not see it as a sign of fatal defect in the Jerusalem congregation.

Peter's decision to enter Cornelius's house set the stage for conflict between the conservative Jewish element (who saw salvation rooted firmly in an acceptance of both Moses and Jesus) and the more progressive wing of the Church (who regarded salvation as a matter of grace apart from law). Peter, in a hastily called meeting of the Jerusalem leadership, had to address the criticism leveled against him. Years later, a group from Jerusalem went to Antioch, a bastion of Gentile Christianity, and taught that circumcision and observance of the customs of Moses were necessary for salvation. Paul and Barnabas traveled to Jerusalem to debate the issue at another meeting of the apostles and elders.

The record of both meetings shows clearly that people who sincerely desire truth cannot avoid conflict, nor need they fear it. Though strong differences existed, respect, reason, and prayer allowed the issues to be discussed and decided. In each case, disagreement was not an indication of weakness in the Church, but proof of its vitality.

Too many people believe that mature Christians don't have disputes with each other, that conflict belongs to the childish. Yet in the latter part of Acts 15, two seasoned Christians had a major disagreement. Barnabas and Paul determined to visit the churches established on their first missionary journey. Barnabas wanted to give John Mark another chance; Paul "did not think it wise." Their disagreement became so heated that one of the greatest missionary teams in Church history split and went separate ways. Listen to the account from the *King James Version*, amplified by using various translations:

> And Barnabas determined to take with them John. . . .
>> was bent on taking (Weymouth)
>> persisted in wanting to take (Williams)
> But Paul thought not good to take him with them. . . .
>> felt that they ought not (TCNT)
>> Paul did not approve (Goodspeed)
>> Paul . . . thought it wrong (Rieu)
> And the contention was so sharp between them,
>> There arose a sharp contention (RSV)
>> an angry feeling (Rotherham)
>> a sharp altercation (Weymouth)
>> They differed so sharply about it (Goodspeed)
>> There was a sharp clash of opinions (Phillips)
>> The disagreement was so sharp (Williams)
> That they departed asunder one from the other.
>> They separated from each other (RSV)
>> They parted company (Moffatt)
>> They went their separate ways (Phillips)
>> It resulted in their separation (Rieu)

Two mature, well-grounded Christians conflicted so sharply that it broke a fruitful partnership. Was either less Christian because of the conflict? Both went on to perform useful work in God's Kingdom in spite of this unfortunate dispute.

Corinthian Christians were familiar with conflict. They had divisions over leadership, legal matters, customs, social standing, and spiritual gifts. Even so, Paul continued to speak of them as "the church of God in Corinth."

The church at Philippi was facing a crucial test of unity when Paul took up his pen to write. Euodia and Syntyche, two women who had worked closely with Paul and each other in the early days of this congregation, were at odds. A close reading of the epistle indicates their contention may have threatened the unity of the whole church. Nevertheless, Paul still longed for this congregation with all "the affection of Christ Jesus."

Conflict was present elsewhere in the Church. The Colossian Christians battled a segment who had "lost hold of the Head." The Thessalonians had to be warned against some of their number who lived in idleness. Timothy was cautioned about those of his flock who would abandon the faith to follow deceiving spirits. John reminded his readers of a group who "went out from us, but did not really belong to us." Were these churches less Christian because they experienced conflict?

It is an easy thing to label conflict as the unmistakable symptom of Spirit-abandoned churches. It is a hard thing to understand that even the most spiritual churches experience dissension. That implies that what distinguishes the Church from the world is not the absence of conflict, but the way conflict is handled. And learning to manage conflict in a Christlike manner is perhaps the hardest thing of all.

ANGER: THE DEADLY SIN?

Christians today find themselves in a curious dilemma. On the one hand, we must acknowledge that conflict was a daily reality in the first-century Church and even in the life of Christ. On the other hand, we feel ashamed of the way the Church of the past and present has handled its conflicts. The ox gores us whichever way we turn: to deny conflict in the Church would be to rewrite much of the New Testament; to acknowledge conflict in the Church would seem to open Pandora's Box.

At the heart of this dilemma is our attitude toward anger. The Church has a long way to go before it comes to grips with this fierce, hot emotion. Like dynamite in the wrong hands, this explosive passion can destroy both the holder and those closest to him.

"Christians don't get angry." Have you heard any good sermons on this lately? They usually take for their text a statement by Jesus in Matthew 5:21-22:

> You have heard that it was said to the people long ago, "Do not murder, and anyone who murders will be subject to judgment." But I tell you that anyone who is angry with his brother will be subject to judgment.

There you have it. Black and white. Christians must not be angry with each other. At the very least, if we *do* become angry it is our Christian duty to hold it in.

But wait! If we take this position we are hard put to reconcile other teachings of the Bible. Psalm 7:11, for instance, speaks of the anger of God. Mark recalls Jesus looking around "with anger" (3:5). All four of the gospels remember Jesus driving the merchants out of the Temple. John places a whip in His hand—hardly the action of an angerless man. And what about all those instances of conflict in the early Church? Were all of them bloodless, passionless affairs, devoid of harsh words and wounded feelings?

When we've finished chewing on these passages, Ephesians 4:26 hits us in the teeth: "Be angry, and yet do not sin" (NASB).

It is as if the ambiguity we feel about anger is also reflected in the Bible's teaching on this subject. Jesus warns against anger, yet we see flashes of it in His own life and in the life of His Church. Paul allows anger in the Christian, but warns that this emotion can easily tempt us to fall into sin. Our black and white melts slowly into shades of gray.

It would be convenient to appeal to the Greek to show that a different word is used in each context. Unfortunately, the same root word (orge) is used in every instance. What sense are we to make of the Bible's teaching in order to discover what our attitude should be toward anger?

Paul's statement leaves no doubt that anger can be experienced without resulting in sin. It may heighten our temptation to sin, but it is not in itself a transgression. If dealt with humbly and quickly, anger need not give the Devil a foothold in our lives. Thus the central issue for Paul is not whether Christians experience negative emotions, but what they do about them. It is the management, not the experience, of anger which concerns Paul.

Actually, Jesus is saying much the same thing in Matthew 5:22. Forbidding anger, He goes on to explain that His interest is not so much in our emotion as in how we behave as a result. "Don't insult people by calling them fools," He insists (the teaching on *raca* in verse 22), and "Settle matters quickly" (the parable of the worshiper and the litigant, verses 23-26).

The Christian is challenged, then, not to eradicate anger from the ranks of the saints, but to sanctify anger through saintly responses. Far from denying or suppressing anger, our challenge is to show the world a constructive way to handle it.

In fact, conflict properly managed has a wealth of associated benefits.

Conflict can strengthen *relationships.* Though conflict begins by threatening the relationship, it can end by deepening it. Peter's love for Jesus was far greater after his angry denial than before. Paul's appreciation for John Mark was deeper in the years that followed their conflict than at any time prior. David's respect for Nathan was heightened rather than weakened by the prophet's confrontation. Though anger has the capacity to destroy relationships, it need not do so. Anger seasoned with the Spirit of Christ can result in greater intimacy. (See Chapter 11.)

There are other benefits of anger as well. A noted writer recently said, "No social advance has been made without dispute."[4] Anger (and the associated conflict) stirs up *the status quo.* It was the clash between Jesus and the Pharisees that split the old wine-skins and made room for new wine. In the same way today, it is usually through struggle that the Church renews its witness to the world.

Anger and conflict also stir our *understanding of the truth.* An impressive thing about the teaching of Jesus is how often He forces people through conflict to reevaluate their understanding of Scripture. In His disputes with the Pharisees, Jesus forced a rethinking of the Sabbath, the resurrection, and the Messiah. The dispute between Jewish and Gentile Christians honed Paul's understanding of salvation by grace through faith. Similarly, a healthy anger forces *us* to reexamine musty traditions in the light of contemporary needs.

Still another value of conflict is the opportunity it affords to *exercise spiritual muscles.* Unexercised muscles become flabby. Spiritual skills gone flat fail us when we need them most. Conflict properly handled produces a Church better prepared to face the world. Confrontations within the safety of God's family ready us for more dangerous confrontations with the forces of evil.

Managed constructively, anger has the potential to deepen our fellowship, freshen our witness, hone our understanding of God's will, and strengthen our hand against Satan. Managed destructively, it has the power to paralyze churches, cripple Christians, and give the world yet one more reason to turn elsewhere for the answers to life.

GETTING A GRIP ON CONFLICT

Some wit has stated that all churches are in one of three stages: (1) They are getting ready to fight; (2) They are fighting; (3) They are getting over a fight.

Like it or not, such is the reality of relationship and the bittersweet confession of the Church as a relationship place. So long as the Church is a place where relationships flourish, it will also be a place where conflicts grow. Relationship and conflict go hand in hand.

Our own experiences validate the truth of this statement. Is there a friendship anywhere that has not had moments of disagreement? Do you know of a marriage that hasn't struggled through periods of discord? Is there a parent alive who hasn't differed strongly with a child? We don't expect such relationships to be free of conflict; we only expect mutual commitment to keep us together as we work through our differences.

Why then are we surprised by conflict in the Church? Why do we recognize the inevitability of conflict in every other loving relationship in our lives, yet balk at clashes among Christians? Perhaps we should apply the same rules to the Church that we do to other relationships: expect conflict, but be committed to working through it together.

Conflict is relationship's Siamese twin. Though nothing would please us more than to enjoy the relationship without the conflict, the two are bound together beyond our ability to divorce them. If you want one you must accept the other.

In fact, we pay for relationships with the sweat it takes

to overcome forces that push us away from each other. Our effort to conquer these forces measures the extent of our love. It is not until we conflict that we discover whether love binds us together or merely convenience.

We must rethink our view of conflict. Conflict is neither a necessary evil nor a signal of defeat. It is simply a reality: Wherever there are people there is conflict. The real issue facing the Church is not how to *avoid* conflict but how to *manage* it. We cannot choose whether to conflict. We can choose to resolve differences when conflicts arise.

DISCUSSION, REFLECTION, AND ACTION

Chapter Discussion

1. In the past six months, have you heard a nonChristian ridicule Christianity because of the way some Christian has behaved? If so, describe what you heard and how you felt.

2. On page 112, the authors point out that the world is not equipped to distinguish between real Christians and those who only say, "Lord, Lord." In light of this, what do you see as the greatest difficulty we face in witnessing?

3. On page 114, the authors say that just because conflict exists in a church does not mean that the Church has lost its way. Do you agree or disagree? Why do you feel that way?

4. Do you feel strongly positive or strongly negative about this statement: "Mature Christians don't have conflicts." Why do you think the way you do?

5. a. What is the major difference between the way the world handles conflict and the way the Church ought to

handle it? (See pages 119-121.)
b. What are some areas of conflict that your group needs to address?
c. How can you deal with these conflicts constructively?

6. Read Mark 3:1-5.
a. How do you think Jesus' anger and your anger differ?
b. Suggest ways of becoming more like Jesus.

7. a. On page 121 the writers state, "Conflict is relationship's Siamese twin." What do you think they mean?
b. How do you feel about this statement?

Personal Bible Search

1. Read Acts 6:1-7.
a. Describe the dispute that arose in the Jerusalem church.
b. Might there have been racial overtones in this conflict? What gives you this impression?
c. How was this dispute settled?
d. What was the result?
e. What truth do you find in this story that you can apply to your own situation? Specifically how is it relevant, and what will you do about it?

2. Read Acts 15:36-41.
a. What difference arose between Paul and Barnabas?
b. How does the text describe the dispute?
c. What was the result?
d. Would you describe these men as mature or immature? Why?

3. Read 2 Timothy 2:14-26.
a. Make a list of the commands given in this passage.

  b. Now mark those that have to do with our interaction
     with each other.
  c. How could following these commands help the local
     church be more united?

Personal Reflection and Action

1. a. What things tend to anger you most?
   b. Why do you think this is so?
   c. What can you do about it?

2. Take a look at your own life. Are you holding on to any old
hurts from the past? If so, write them down: describe what
happened and how you felt. Then ask God to enable you to
forgive the person who hurt you (it may take some time
before you feel able to do this). When you are finished,
destroy the paper as a sign that you are letting go of that old
bitterness and choosing to forgive, even though the other
person was wrong.

3. Do you know any brother or sister who has been hurt by a
past dispute and so has drawn back from trusting others? If
so, look for ways to love this person so that he or she can
begin to trust and accept fellowship.

CHAPTER NINE

Heart-to-Heart Combat

Consider the lowly pup tent. Canvas and poles and rope strung together in delicate balance. When properly erected, a marvel of strength and shelter. When poorly assembled, an accident waiting for a place to happen. Though each component is important, the poles are what gives the tent its strength and shape. Two poles are necessary for a pup tent to stand, two poles always in tension if the tent is to attain the shape its designer intended. Too little tension and the tent sags; too much and it rips apart.

At times a pup tent reminds us of nothing so much as the Church. It too is a delicate balance of various elements, offering either strength and shelter or potential problems. Important activities form the canvas of the Church. But like the tent, the shape and strength of the Church derive from the two poles which hold it up: *people* and *principles*.

Certain *principles* tie the Church together, ideas that Christians share in common and that distinguish the Church from the host of other groups meeting in town. Faith in God, acceptance of Jesus as Lord and Savior, a sense of mission, and a commitment to worship and good works are some of the fundamental principles that transform diverse people into a unified Christian community. Without principles to believe in, there could be no Church.

People are equally important to the Church. Churches are not buildings where strangers occasionally gather to meditate in public solitude. The Church is a community of people whose lives are intertwined by divine intent. We love each other. We call one another "brother" and "sister." We share struggles and confess sin and pool resources and combine faith. Without people to build on, there could be no Church.

Both people and principles are necessary to the survival of the Church. But they do not stand easily together. Like the tent, there must be a certain tension between these poles if the Church is to attain the shape intended by its designer.

Principles, by definition, pull in the direction of unanimity: they insist on agreement and similarity of thinking. People, on the other hand, pull in the direction of diversity: they assert the importance of individuality and variation. Principles ask us to think. People want us to feel. Principles have to do with vertical issues. People call us to horizontal concerns. Principles are the stuff of philosophy. People are the stuff of psychology. Getting the tension right is an arduous job indeed.

Part of the Church always sags when you throw out one of the poles. Those concerned primarily with principle will work to ensure that their beliefs are advanced even at the expense of relationships. Those primarily committed to people will sacrifice principle so that relationships are not damaged. Those who value both principle and people equally struggle to keep a healthy tension between the two poles and to find a path that sacrifices neither their faith nor their fellows.

It so happens that most problems with churches can be analyzed by looking at the tension between these two poles.

The methods, strategies, and styles of people in conflict are governed by their commitments to people on the one hand and to principles on the other. These two commitments determine to a large degree the attitudes and goals we bring to a conflict situation.

THE CONFLICT GRID

The "Conflict Grid" has become a popular way of visualizing and analyzing the way people fight (see Figure 1).

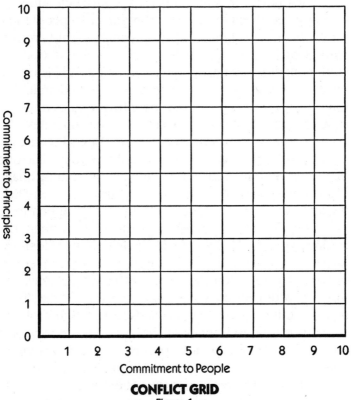

CONFLICT GRID
Figure 1

Authors in the fields of management, psychotherapy, and theology have utilized this grid to explain why we conflict as we do. The grid is built around the two commitments we have just discussed: The poles of our tent are laid at right angles and become the axes of the conflict grid.

The horizontal axis depicts our commitment to people. Notice that such a commitment can be low, high, or somewhere in between (the greater the number on the axis, the stronger the commitment). In the same way, the vertical axis shows the strength of our commitment to principles.

At least five different conflict styles can be identified by knowing the strength of our commitment to people and principles. The strength of those commitments predicts with great accuracy the way we approach conflict. Little commitment to either people or principles gives rise to entirely different conflict strategies than great commitment to both. A primary concern for people motivates different styles of fighting than a primary concern for principles.

All of us fall somewhere on this grid. As we discuss each of these five positions, you will probably see yourself in one of the descriptions. You will certainly see the spitting image of someone you know! Before reading further, you will find it helpful to take the Conflict Styles Inventory (Appendix A, page 209). This survey is adapted from an instrument developed by Norman Shawchuck[1] and is a means of identifying where you fit on the conflict grid. Answer the inventory questions, grade yourself according to the directions, and discover your primary and secondary conflict styles. Then return to this chapter and read the descriptions that follow.

It is crucial to remember that each of these styles is appropriate for certain situations. None of them is inherently evil. It would be wonderful if each of us could choose the style most appropriate for the conflict facing us. Unfortunately, most of us are stuck with one style which we tend to use in any and every conflict. In coping with past conflicts, we have learned a set of behaviors and attitudes that seem to work. This set becomes our conflict style which we rely on whether it is appropriate or not.

All five conflict styles have their place and use, but only one recommends itself as a consistently effective means of managing Church conflict. While four of these styles provide all-too-accurate descriptions of the way we usually handle conflict, only one challenges us to a mode of action that is Christlike to the core.

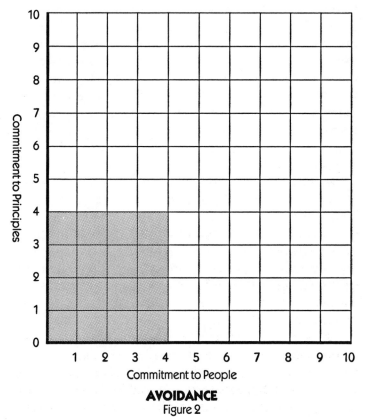

AVOIDANCE
Figure 2

AVOIDANCE

When we lack significant commitments to both the people of the Church and the principles of the Church, we are apt to use *avoidance* as a primary means of dealing with conflict (see Figure 2). Our fear of conflict outweighs any commitment to relationships or doctrine, and we seek only the illusory peace that comes from escape. Avoiders, like the tortoise, pull into their shells at the first sign of discord.

Avoidance takes many forms. It can be as mild as silent passivity in the face of a conflict, or as strong as fleeing the situation for "greener grass." Whatever the form, the message is the same: the avoider will not take the risk of inserting himself into the conflict situation. He does not care enough about the people or the principles involved to invest himself in a resolution of the disagreement.

Certainly there are conflicts that can be safely avoided. Some issues are simply too trivial to merit attention, while others are too distant to raise our concern. Not every conflict demands our participation.

But when avoidance becomes our style of choice in the face of conflict, something is wrong. There are certain principles for which all Christians should be willing to fight. And for each of us there should be certain people on whose behalf we would gladly do battle. Avoidance of conflict at all cost is not a sign of our love for peace; it is only an indication of our lack of love for anything else.

COMPROMISE

Few conflict styles have as bad a reputation among religious people as *compromise.* The word sets visions of "selling out" dancing in our heads. Many perceive compromise as only a more subtle form of avoidance, where settling matters quickly becomes more important than settling matters well.

The following story captures the essence of our suspicions about compromising on religious issues. A hunter, desiring a fur coat for the winter, enters a woods in search of a bear. Meanwhile, a bear, preparing for hibernation, goes into the woods in search of a meal. As fate would have it, the hunter and the bear meet. The hunter takes aim at the bear and is about to shoot when the bear says, "Wait a minute! Let's talk this over. Maybe we can work out a compromise. Come sit on this log beside me."

The hunter, being a reasonable man, agrees to discuss the matter, and sits on the log beside the bear. It does not take them long to work out a compromise: The bear had his meal, and the hunter got his fur coat.

Compromise *does* imply a willingness to make certain sacrifices. Because the compromiser values both principles and people (see Figure 3) to a moderate degree, he sacrifices a little of each in order to save the bulk of both. The message communicated by this style is, "We care enough about people to sacrifice a little truth and enough about truth to sacrifice a few people." It is the delicate balance between the two which the compromiser works to maintain. Compromise is the preferred style of the politician, providing "each side with a little bit of winning in order to persuade each to accept a little bit of losing."[2]

For many conflicts in the Church, compromise is not an appropriate solution. Solomon solved the dilemma of two women claiming the same child by offering half the child to each woman—a compromise if ever there were one! It is interesting to note, however, that the woman who refused to agree to this compromise was awarded the baby. Babies—like certain principles—lose something when divided down the middle.

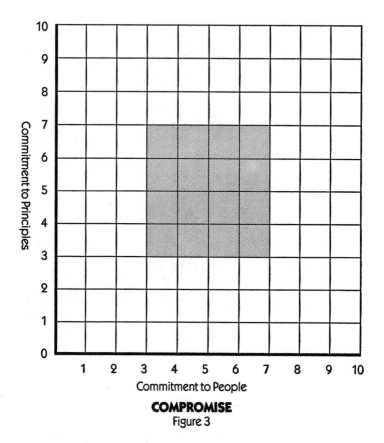

COMPROMISE
Figure 3

However, there are many times in Church conflict when compromise is not only appropriate but vital. Most churches do not struggle on a daily basis with great, non-negotiable theological or moral issues. Our primary difficulties arise from stubborn personalities unyielding on matters of far less importance. Compromise is a legitimate approach to many problems facing local congregations.

The early Church found compromise a useful and practical tool. The Jerusalem Council (Acts 15) resolved a serious issue through compromise. What should Jewish Christians expect of Gentile converts? Though the apostles and the elders of the Jerusalem church did not require Gentiles to become practicing Jews, they did bind upon them abstinence "from food sacrificed to idols, from blood, from the meat of strangled animals and from sexual immorality" (Acts 15:29).

While forbidding sexual sins was completely in line with Jesus' teachings, the other issues seem to spring more from a compromise with the Jewish contingent of the Church. These practices were particularly repulsive to Christians raised under the law of Moses. Though Paul would later state, "I am fully convinced that no food is unclean in itself" (Romans 14:14), he fully concurred with the compromise of the Jerusalem Council and reaffirmed his stance to both the Roman and the Corinthian churches.[3]

Compromise can be used in solving Church conflicts, and probably should have a wider application than it does at present. The important thing is that we be careful when we compromise—we must ensure that we are sitting on a log with a pussy cat rather than a bear.

COMPETITION

The competitor (see Figure 4) is strong in his commitment to principle but relatively weak on commitment to people. When conflicts arise, the competitor's natural bent is to defend "the principle of the thing" without great regard for the feelings and ideas of others. Such a one finds it easier to sacrifice people than to question the status quo.

Competition is built around the use of power. Whether the conflict is over large issues or small, the competitor uses authority and the threat of sanctions to bring disagreement to an acceptable end.

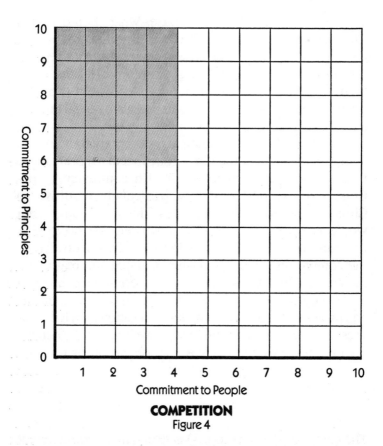

COMPETITION
Figure 4

In its mildest form, this style involves the paternalism of a leader who purports to know what is best for all concerned. At its worst, an individual becomes "aggressive, domineering, and generally uncooperative in the pursuit of any solution except his/her own."[4] At all levels, the competitor suppresses disagreement through power, control, and manipulation.

In defense of this style we should note there are certain issues over which the Church must be willing to fight. The

Apostle Paul considered salvation by grace through faith to be such an issue when he faced an element in the Church that wanted to bind Mosaic legislation on Gentile believers. He was willing to battle these Judaizing teachers, calling them "dogs" and "mutilators of the flesh" (Philippians 3:2) and wishing that in their obsession with circumcision they would "go the whole way and emasculate themselves" (Galatians 5:12).

However, not every issue faced by the Church is quite so clear-cut. The vast majority of concerns fall into gray areas where room exists for legitimate debate and sincere differences. When the competitor fails to make this distinction and uses the same strategies to force his way on carpeting the foyer that he would use in defending the Trinity, trouble is bound to result. Paul warned the Romans not to pass "judgment on disputable matters," and not to "destroy your brother" (Romans 14:1,15) for the sake of food or drink or other questionable issues.

Unfortunately, the competitor is no more adept at modifying his style to fit the situation than we are; he tends to use his competitive style regardless of its appropriateness to the issues in question. He is not indifferent to those who disagree with him, nor does he wish to exclude them—he simply places prime importance on his personal perceptions and values and will broach no diversity where such matters are concerned.

The outcome of a persistent use of this competitive style is clear: heated emotions, wounded people, and an ever-shrinking circle of fellowship. When the principles are central, competition may be an appropriate course of action. But in the vast majority of cases, competitive strategies serve only to suppress diversity, enforce uniformity, and concentrate power in the hands of those who are most demanding.

COMPLIANCE

If we say that the competitor is high in his commitment to principle and relatively low in his commitment to people, then the complier can be described as just the opposite (see Figure 5). When conflict arises, the complier will almost always lean toward preserving relationship at the cost of principle.

As with each of the styles we have discussed so far, *compliance* has a place in the functioning of the Church. Again, Paul provides us with an excellent example of this approach to conflict. Although he would not allow Titus (a Gentile convert) to be circumcised, and though he warned the Galatians that if they let themselves be circumcised, "Christ will be of no value" to them (Galatians 5:2), he nonetheless circumcised Timothy "because of the Jews who lived in that area" (Acts 16:3). Paul complied with the wishes of his fellow Jews as a matter of expediency so that his work among that group might be more effective. He sacrificed a lesser principle for the sake of a greater fellowship.

Many, however, choose compliance because they *always* view principle as more expendable than people. "Having everyone get along together," they think, "is more important than any issue over which we could differ." With such people, relationship must be preserved at all cost. Conflict, for the complier, is always a greater evil than capitulation.

As a result, disagreements are downplayed and smoothed over. Surface harmony is maintained by conceding to the wishes of others and complying with whatever conditions will keep the group together. "Doctrine divides, love unites" is the rallying cry of Christians stuck in the compliance mode.

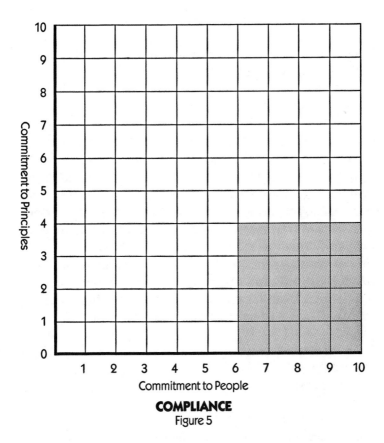

COMPLIANCE
Figure 5

When the desire to avoid confrontation is the primary goal brought to all conflict situations, relationship always supercedes conviction. If compliance is the only style of conflict we use, truth will be sacrificed consistently for the sake of tranquility. Over time, the group which relies on compliance to settle its differences will inevitably wander from the principles on which it was initially founded.

This is precisely what happened at the foot of Mount Sinai with the Israelites. Moses had been on the mountain for many days, and the people were restless for leadership. Just at the moment Aaron should have stepped out boldly to confront the sinful request of the Israelites, he complied with their appeal and built a golden calf for them to worship. Later, justifying to Moses what he had done, Aaron implied that his actions were merely intended to keep peace.

When peace is purchased at any price, the Church finds itself building golden calves of its own. Though fellowship might be maintained, it is only a hollow association. Any group that sacrifices fundamental convictions on the altar of unity eventually becomes a union that has lost its reason for existence. Too many in the Christian tradition have done just that, opting for accommodation when what was needed was an affirmation of our most cherished beliefs.

Before moving on, there is one comment we must make regarding the two conflict styles we have just discussed, competition and compliance. *In the final analysis, these two styles of conflicting are houses built on shifting sand.*

If our analysis is correct, competition stems from high regard for principle and relatively low regard for people. The competitor often justifies a harsh and authoritarian approach to conflict by insisting he is only upholding the principles of God. One question immediately comes to mind, however: "How can you have a high regard for God's principles yet disregard the principles God gave about the way we treat people?"

"Considering others better than yourselves" is also one of God's principles. "Live in harmony with one another" is an important precept. The command to "Accept him whose faith is weak, without passing judgment on disputable matters" is one of the decrees we are bound to honor.[5]

Those of us who only want to uphold God's holy principles—what have we done about Paul's instruction to "clothe yourselves with compassion, kindness, humility, gentleness and patience"? How will we respond to the call to "make every effort to do what leads to peace and mutual edification"? Have we read that the fruit of the Spirit often takes the form of love, peace, patience, kindness, and gentleness?[6]

These commands are as legitimate and binding as any other "Thou shalt" or "Thou shalt not" recorded in the Bible. Someone truly committed to *all* of God's principles would be the last person in the world to sacrifice people as a solution to conflict.

The same kind of reasoning holds true with the complier. We have stated that the consistent use of accommodation stems from a high regard for people and a relatively low regard for principle. The complier often justifies downplaying doctrine by insisting he is protecting people's feelings and diversity. Again, a question comes to mind: "How can you have such a high regard for God's people yet disregard what God Himself says is necessary for fullness of life?"

We can't claim to love people when we lack the courage to hold them to the principles God has given for their benefit. Specific teaching on "Do not conform any longer to the pattern of this world" is also an act of love. Paul was not deficient in compassion when he commanded the Corinthians to expel an immoral brother, and then went on to insist that homosexuals, the greedy, drunkards, and slanderers would not inherit the Kingdom of God. When James asserts that faith without works is dead, he isn't showing callousness to nominal Christians, but rather loving them enough to call them to real discipleship.[7]

Those of us who want to maintain a warm and accepting fellowship—what have we done to ensure it is foremost a *Christian* fellowship? Does the Church truly serve people by neglecting to call them to a clear, Christlike ethic? Can we develop godly and happy homes by side-stepping the issue of mutual submission simply because it upsets many of our members? We do not give people what leads to full life by telling them, "It doesn't matter what you believe, so long as you *do* believe," or by teaching that the road Jesus said was narrow and hard is, in fact, broad and easy.

Preaching and requiring obedience to God's principles is as much an act of love as serving and forgiving and accepting. In fact, helping people live according to God's standards does more honest good for people—both now and in the hereafter—than all the unconditional acceptance you care to heap upon them. Someone truly committed to God's people would be the last person in the world to sacrifice principles in order to maintain harmony.

CAREFRONTING

Avoidance is often a cop-out. Compromise works best only with issues that, in the end, don't really matter. Competitive approaches doom us to eternal warfare. Compliance forever condemns us to spineless acquiescence.

Is there a way to fight in the Church that preserves our respect for both diversity and doctrine? Surely we can approach conflict without having to determine *a priori* whom we are willing to sacrifice or what we are willing to scrap! In trying to make this tent stand strong and straight, we must find a proper tension between its two poles without sawing one or the other in half.

The final conflict style attempts to achieve this delicate balance. The "carefronter" (see Figure 6), unlike practitioners of each of the styles discussed so far, has an *absolute* commitment to both people and principles; he is unwilling to sacrifice either in his efforts to manage conflict. The carefronter sees conflict resolution not as an exercise in compromise nor as a battle to be won or lost, but as a process in which God's people and God's principles are brought together—each to test and validate the other.

The term *carefronting* is borrowed from David Augsburger, who understands this attitude to be a combination of love and power.

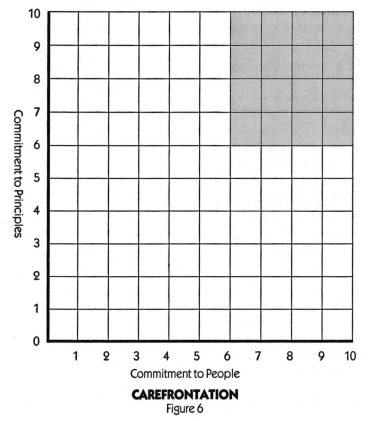

CAREFRONTATION
Figure 6

Carefronting unifies concern for relationship with concerns for goals. So one can have something to stand for [goals] as well as someone to stand with [relationship] without sacrificing one for the other, or collapsing one into another. Thus one can love powerfully and be powerfully loving. These are not contradictory. They are complementary.[8]

Jesus was a carefronter. He was able to exemplify this absolute commitment to both the will of God and the people of God. He would not pit the two against each other, as if God could defend this side against that.

A classic example of Christ in conflict is found in John 8—the story of the woman caught in adultery. The Pharisees tried to put Jesus in the awkward position of choosing people or principle—either side with the woman (and against God's explicit teaching) or side with the Law (and condemn the woman to death): "In the Law Moses commanded us to stone such women. Now what do you say?"

Jesus refused to see the two as opposing forces working against each other. He could acknowledge the woman was a sinner deserving death (and thus defend the righteousness of the Law). Without blinking an eye, however, He could go on to insist the same was true of each individual standing there (and so argue for humanity's need for compassion). With the words, "Let him who is without sin among you . . ." Jesus shifted the focus away from the Law's demand for punishment to the Law's provision for mercy.

He repeated this method in later speaking to the woman. With the statement "I do not condemn you," Jesus showed His compassion for her, yet with the words "Go, and sin no more," Jesus indicated His continuing commitment to God's ethical standards.

Did anyone leave the Temple that day (least of all the woman) confused about Jesus' stance on immorality? Did He somehow downplay the seriousness of sin, or encourage others to take adultery lightly? Not at all. Jesus showed clearly His commitment to the principles of God. But neither did anyone leave the Temple thinking that people were unimportant in the face of God's Law. Jesus showed with equal clarity His commitment to people.

On this occasion, Jesus refused to deal with conflict by sacrificing either people or principle. He affirmed God's principle in a way that protected a woman who was precious to God. Both were important. Neither was expendable.

Carefronting is calling people to submit themselves to God's principles. It is the clear, firm enunciation of God's will as revealed through God's Word. It is the unashamed and unhesitating advocacy of an absolute discipleship involving the cross and the lordship of Jesus. Carefronting is all that. But it is done in the spirit of meekness, spoken with the words of humility, shown through personal example. Carefronting is preaching with a washbasin in hand and a towel about the waist. It is the art of holding firmly to God's commands while still considering others better than yourself. It is the difficult task of walking the high-wire of God's expectations without the benefits of a safety net woven from self-righteousness. Carefronting is prophecy coupled with patience, holiness balanced with hope, law washed down with large ladles of love.

Carefronting is something else as well. It is trusting that God can work through other people. It is acknowledging in others a commitment to God that equals or even excels our own. It is the humility to accept that we have no monopoly on God's truth, and that differences in interpretation do not always signify differences in spiritual passion. Carefronting is the willingness to learn from one another, to be led into a deeper understanding of God's truth by a deeper appreciation of each other's perspectives. It sees diversity as a strength and is not threatened by disagreement. It values conflict as an opportunity to listen afresh to God's voice.

Carefronting is risking comfortable positions in the crucible of new and perhaps more godly insights. It is the freedom to change without the worry of who gets credit for being right.

The message communicated by the carefronter is "I'm so committed to our principles that I will not compromise them simply to arrive at some temporary peace. On the other hand, I am so committed to you that I will not sacrifice you simply to avoid questioning or rethinking my principles. The only solution I will accept is the one that protects both God's people and God's principles."

That is carefronting—a unique, delicate blending of commitments that enables the carefronter to keep the proper tension in a church torn between the diversity of its members and the importance of its principles. We see that tension in the life of Jesus as He patiently molds twelve rough and imperfect men into a team that will turn the world upside down. We see it in God Himself as He balances the judgment of His righteousness with the compassion of His love. People and principle. Mercy and judgment. Love and ideals. Always the tension.

Too many of our churches have lost that tension, and as a result our tents sag. We've either suppressed our love of people or doused our passion for God's Word or simply cut away too much on both poles. Whatever the problem, the result is always the same: The Church loses its shape. She hangs slack. Every wind that blows rattles through her rigging and tears at those still huddled in her corners.

It is time that Christians commit once more to both poles of the Church. As we conflict, we must endeavor to maintain the tension that allows God's Church to achieve the shape intended by its Designer. Such balance comes only through continual exposure to Jesus Christ. Only He can take our avoiding-compromising-competing-complying spirits and teach us how to speak the truth in love.

DISCUSSION, REFLECTION, AND ACTION

Chapter Discussion

The discussion for this chapter should be built around the "Conflict Styles Inventory" found in Appendix A.

1. Make sure that each member has completed and scored the inventory. (If necessary, allow time for this now.)

2. Reproduce the grid of Box 1 on markerboard, poster-board, or a large sheet of paper.

3. Ask each person to share:
   • what his or her prevalent style seems to be;
   • how he or she felt about doing the inventory. (Some people hate surveys, others may have had trouble deciding how to answer, and others may have found the exercise helpful in understanding themselves. Give everyone a chance to express his or her feelings.)

4. Place a dot or write a name at the spot on your grid where the inventory placed each member.

5. What do the results of this grid tell you about yourselves as individuals and as a group? What other reactions do you have about this exercise?

Personal Bible Search

1. Read Ephesians 4:14-16.
   a. What characteristic of children is Paul concerned with in this passage?
   b. How must truth be spoken? Give some very specific examples of how you think this should work in practice. (Draw on situations that have occurred among

group members, if you can.)
c. How does the Body build itself up?

2. Read 1 Peter 3:15-16.
   a. Before we answer someone's questions, Peter says we should "in [our] hearts set apart Christ as Lord." Why do you think this is crucial?
   b. In your own words, describe the manner in which Peter says we should answer people's questions.

3. Look again at 2 Timothy 2:22-26.
   a. What is the product of "foolish and stupid arguments"?
   b. How should a servant of God deal with those who oppose him? How would this work in practice?

Personal Reflection and Action

1. Try to fit the instructions from the passages you studied in "Personal Bible Search" into the grid. Which character qualities and instructions reflect "Commitment to Principle"? Which ones reflect "Commitment to People"?

   Example: Speaking the truth is on the side of principle. What about love (Ephesians 4:15)?

2. After comparing these passages to the grid, how biblically sound do you think the grid is?

3. For the next week, pay attention to how you handle conflicts that arise. Do you act the way the inventory suggested you would? Do you think your reactions are godly? Explain.

CHAPTER TEN

"Lord, Teach Us to Fight"

On one side of a great river, the forest was ablaze. Animals fell over each other, racing to the water and to the safety of the other shore.

Now it came to pass that a scorpion and a turtle arrived at the water's edge. Since he was not much of a swimmer, the scorpion turned to the turtle and made this request:

"Sir, would you allow me to ride on your back as you cross this river? The water is too deep and the current is too strong for me to swim to the other shore."

The turtle replied, "I will not let you on my back! No sooner would I get to the middle of the river than you would sting me and I would die."

The scorpion responded calmly, "Now, that would not be a logical thing for me to do. It would be a very unreasonable thing, in fact. If I stretched out my tail to sting you and you died in the middle of the river, I would die also."

"You are quite right," said the turtle, after giving some thought to the scorpion's statement. "I will give you a ride across the river." And with that, the turtle allowed the scorpion to climb onto his back and launched out into the current.

When the turtle had battled his way to midstream, the

scorpion turned, lifted his tail, and stung the turtle where he was most vulnerable—in the extended portion of the neck.

The poor turtle began to gasp and flop as the poison spread through his body. Sinking into the river, he shouted at the scorpion in unbelief and despair, "Why did you do such a stupid and illogical thing?"

"Logic?" replied the scorpion as he, too, slipped beneath the tide. "Logic has nothing to do with it. *It's my nature to sting!*"

THE SCORPIONS AMONG US

What is your nature? Especially when conflicts arise, what aspect of your personality comes to the fore? When the going gets tough, what part of you really gets going?

In the last chapter, we discussed conflict styles. We noted that most of us have learned one method of fighting that—for better or worse—tends to be our style of choice when conflict confronts us. Some of us are like the tortoise—withdrawing into our shells at the first sign of conflict. Some of us, like chameleons, change colors and blend into the crowd.

Many of us, however, are more like the scorpion. Despite good intentions and promises to behave, we sting and bite when faced with people who do not see things our way. As soon as conflicts arise, logic abandons its past resolution and our poisonous tongues seize control.

This chapter is for the scorpions in our congregations. Of the conflict styles discussed in Chapter 9, none does more noticeable damage to the Church than the competitive style. By definition, competitive strategies alienate brothers and sisters, hurting feelings and wounding relationships. Whenever we sacrifice people in an attempt to resolve conflict, the Church becomes a battle zone and the ultimate casualty of its own tactics.

Actually, this chapter is for the scorpion in *each* of us. None of us is above playing the competitor. No matter what our predominant style of conflict management may be, the scorpion lurks just below the surface in us all. Given the right issue, even the meekest Christian can turn into a poisonous competitor, stinging first and only later repenting of words and actions that seem completely out of character.

THE WIN-LOSE CONFLICT STRATEGY

Call us scorpions or call us competitors—the basic strategy in the heat of battle is the same. Conflict is seen as a win/lose situation where only the strong survive. It's the fight-or-flight, us-versus-them mentality that infects like a virus when combat looms.

No *modus operandi* comes more naturally to us during times of discord than the *win/lose* mode of conflict behavior. Competing against and defeating an opponent is our society's most prevalent strategy of interpersonal interaction. Win/lose terms fill the language of business, politics, education, and even religion. One "wins" a promotion or a raise, "beats" the opposition, "outsmarts" a teacher, and "thrashes" an opponent. In a society that stresses winning, it is no wonder competitive behavior abounds even where it is not appropriate.

The Church is not immune to this competitive mindset. When conflicts arise, it is not unusual for members to interrupt each other, voice their own ideas without listening to others, and form power blocks rallying around their position and opposing that of others. Such power struggles, characteristic of the win/lose orientation, destroy the fellowship of the Church. When one group determines to *win* at the expense of other Church members, the "tie that binds" is strained. The original purpose of the Church becomes overshadowed by the struggle to triumph.

Even when the battle is over, the win/lose tactic ensures that victory is bittersweet.

> Adoption of a win/lose strategy not only affects the tactics that one adopts in conflict, it even affects the way in which one sizes up the outcome of the disagreement. "Winners" are losers because they can hardly savor their ill-gotten gains; and "losers" are bitter and steeled for later battles in which they can balance the books. It has long been recognized that one can win or lose a dispute; but, the loser can accept or reject the defeat.[1]

No one wins. The loser in a win/lose situation has little motivation to implement the victors' plans and programs. He resents the winner's control over the future, having had no chance to contribute his resources to the problem-solving process.

Conversely, the winner finds it hard to enforce his ideas. Cohesion has been destroyed, communication remains limited and inaccurate, and members suspect and resent each other. The competitive win/lose way of dealing with controversy sabotages all aspects of Church effectiveness. It attacks the heart of Church unity by undercutting the cooperation needed among members.

The outcomes of a win/lose situation are predictable. The Church polarizes into an us-them attitude. Brothers and sisters dominate and intimidate others for whom Christ died. Members frequently deny the legitimacy of the ideas and interests of others and consider only their own needs. They undermine others' positions while augmenting their own. The consequences of such strategies invariably are broken relationships and wounded souls.

Though something may be gained through these tactics, the gains are short-lived. The negative consequences provoked are destined to last much longer. In the end, everyone loses in the win/lose pattern.

THE WIN/WIN ALTERNATIVE

Most of us have come to view conflict as a *threat* to relationships rather than an *encouragment* to them. It is difficult for us to imagine anything positive resulting from discord—which only goes to show how steeped we are in the win/lose tradition.

Fortunately, there is a way to manage conflict that leads to greater levels of fraternity and holds the promise of deeper relationships. Conflict doesn't *necessarily* result in estrangement. It *can* open the door to true intimacy.

The *win/win* mode provides a real and hopeful alternative to the win/lose strategy described above. It is a tactic stressing cooperation rather than competition. Though this style of conflict management is less natural, it is certainly more beneficial in the context of the Church.

As we discuss this alternative, you might think it is nothing but pie-in-the-sky naivete. You may appreciate it in theory, but doubt its applicability to real life. Yet the win/win mindset is just another way of describing the carefronting style of conflict management. When we explore this alternative way of dealing with conflict, we are actually studying the approach to conflict Jesus Himself predominantly used.

The contention here is that the win/win, carefronting style is the method Jesus identified as characteristic of those who would be His true disciples. Unless we find a way to make this strategy a reality in our churches, we will be doomed to repeat the mistakes of past conflicts.

For any church to function effectively, cooperation among members must receive high priority. At no time is this more imperative than in the midst of conflict. Without a concerted effort toward cooperation among members, there can be no coordination of behavior, no communication, and no interaction that strengthens the local church rather than tearing it apart. Most importantly, without cooperation there is no hope of resolving conflict in a manner that preserves and promotes the unity of the church.

Cooperation is the most important and basic form of human interaction, and by far the most important characteristic of effective churches.

The win/win method of conflict management deals with controversy openly and honestly. It sees conflict not as a war to be won but as an opportunity to promote the good of all. The goal of this approach is not to polarize a church but to deal with conflict in a unified and mutually beneficial manner. The objective is to make everyone a winner, thus helping all aspects of congregational effectiveness.

When members approach controversy from a win/win point of view, they more often are able to recognize the legitimacy of one another's interests and to search for a solution accommodating the needs of all. Problem solving rather than problem suppression becomes the aim. They try to influence one another through persuasion and patience, working to build up mutual power rather than personal power.

The win/win mode of conflict management is constructive for several reasons:

1. It allows us to keep constantly in mind who is the enemy and who is the ally. Our brothers and sisters

are not the enemy in this spiritual battle we fight. To treat one another generously during conflict is a victory in itself—to abuse one another, no matter what the issue, is itself a defeat.

2. It strengthens the chances for finding a high-quality solution to the disagreement. When the church through discussion and communication arrives at a solution, it will more likely be a true remedy than a stopgap measure. Ideas hammered on the public anvil are always stronger than those hatched behind closed doors.

3. It increases every member's motivation to implement the decisions of the group. Because the interests and thoughts of each have been considered, each is more willing to support the group's decision. Once we have decided something *as a group,* there is no need for an enforcer to come around, stand over us with a baseball bat and say, "I am the authority here. You will comply with my wishes because I won and you lost." Solutions decided *by* a few and *for* a few are often left *to* the few to implement.

4. It promotes relationships rather than destroying them. A conflict culminating with winners and losers leaves festering feelings of resentment. There are no "good winners"—all winners are insufferable in the eyes of those who lost. And there are no "gracious losers"—all losers are continually suspect in the eyes of those who won. Only a humility which makes winners of all allows a church to thrive after a fight.

God expects the local church to work through differences in a manner that protects people, preserves principles, promotes peace, and perpetuates partnership. Nothing is more needed in the Church today than a spirit which ensures that differences in opinions, ideas, values, beliefs and goals are approached from a cooperative win/win orientation rather than a competitive win/lose mode.

JESUS THE FIGHTER

Jesus was no stranger to conflict. Some conflicts were thrust upon Him; others He initiated. But whatever the source of controversy, Jesus consistently favored a strategy of conflict that protected both principles and people. He was a proponent of the carefronting, win/win mode of conflict resolution.

As we study the example of Jesus in conflict situations, it is important to remember that in at least one respect, Jesus was very different from us. He was always right! He saw the will of God absolutely and knew God's mind completely. We, on the other hand, "see but a poor reflection" and can only "know in part" (1 Corinthians 13:12).

Accordingly, certain aspects of Christ's conflict style are *not* to be imitated by His disciples. We cannot take the role of teacher and Lord in conflict situations (as He could). We cannot speak with absolute confidence and omniscience (as He did). We cannot see the hearts of others and know with certainty their motives (as He had the ability to do).

There are, however, some characteristics of Christ in conflict we would do well to imitate. In particular, there are lessons for us to learn in the attitude Jesus took toward those with whom He clashed. At the heart of Jesus' conflict style was a firm commitment to win people rather than arguments. Though He certainly won the arguments (because He was certainly right), He did it in such a way that people were not sacrificed.

The best example of this was His relationship with Simon Peter. Jesus and Simon had several intense conflicts. But Jesus always found a way to protect Simon, even in the midst of their frequent confrontations. Simon didn't like the idea of putting the nets out again after a long night of fishing (Luke 5:1-11). When the great catch of fish threatened to sink Simon's boat, he urged Jesus, "Go away from me, Lord; I am a sinful man." But Jesus did not go away. He called headstrong, opinionated Simon to be a fisher of men, one of the Twelve.

When Jesus began to tell His disciples about His coming death, "Peter took him aside and began to rebuke him" (Mark 8:32). Jesus used exceedingly strong language in turn to rebuke Peter: "Get behind me, Satan! You do not have in mind the things of God, but the things of men" (verse 33). Yet Jesus did not reject Peter, only correct him. Six days later, Jesus chose the inner circle of the apostles to witness His transfiguration—Peter was still included among the favored three (Mark 9:2).

On the night He was betrayed, Jesus tried to wash Peter's feet, only to be rebuffed by Peter's emphatic "You shall never wash my feet" (John 13:8). Jesus had to insist, "Unless I wash you, you have no part with me." When Jesus told His disciples He was about to go where they could not follow, Peter asserted he would go anywhere with Jesus, even if it meant laying down his life (John 13:37). Jesus had to break the news to Peter that he would, that very evening, deny even knowing Jesus. In the garden, Peter slept while Jesus sweat blood. A disappointed Jesus asked, "Simon. . . . Could you not keep watch for one hour?" (Mark 14:37). As Jesus was being arrested, Peter lashed out with a sword and was told in no uncertain terms, "Put your sword away! Shall I not drink the cup the Father has given me?" Within hours Peter stood by a fire, swearing by everything holy that he did not know the Man (Mark 14:66-72). It must have been the worst night of Peter's life. As it ended, Peter was left broken and sobbing.

But even after all this, Jesus did not wash His hands of Simon Peter. Christ rebuked and corrected and confronted him untold times, but He never threw him away. The patience and gentleness of Jesus is nowhere more evident than in His dealing with Peter after the Resurrection. What a world of meaning lies between the lines when angels commanded the women to tell the "disciples *and Peter*" (Mark 16:7, emphasis added) that Jesus would be waiting for them in Galilee, or when Paul hinted that Jesus appeared to Peter privately before appearing to the other disciples (1 Corinthians 15:5). And how much poorer we would be had John not recorded that poignant scene by the Sea of Galilee where the resurrected Jesus made sure that Peter knew there was still a place for him in the work of the Kingdom (John 21:15-19).

Jesus advocated this win/win attitude not only by His example but by His teaching. His lessons on forgiving as often as needed (Luke 17:3-4), reconciling with a brother quickly (Matthew 5:23-26), doing so privately (Matthew 18:15), and taking the initiative regardless of who is in the wrong (cf. Matthew 5:23, 18:15) underscore Christ's concern with resolving conflict in a win/win manner.

Jesus often rejected the win/lose thinking of others. When His disciples argued over who was the greatest (certainly a win/lose conflict), Jesus emphasized that such thinking was characteristic of the "Gentiles," not of those who would be His disciples. Rather, they would show their greatness through service and humility (Luke 22:24-27). And when James and John wanted to call down fire on a Samaritan village which had denied them shelter for the evening (a win/lose solution if ever there was one), Jesus rebuked them and walked on to the next village (Luke 9:51-56).

In fairness, there were times when Jesus employed win/lose language in His conflicts with others. Especially in His confrontations with the Pharisees (see Matthew 23, for example), Jesus made it abundantly clear that He was right and they were tragically wrong. But such language was reserved for those who "shut the kingdom of heaven in men's faces" (Matthew 23:13), who rejected the good news that He came to offer (Matthew 21:33-46), and who "let go of the commandments of God" to hold on "to the traditions of men" (Mark 7:6-8). Never did Jesus conflict in this way with His disciples or those sincerely searching for the Kingdom of God.

In fact, when Jesus taught His disciples how to handle conflict, He often insisted that it was better to lose than to win at the expense of others. Rather than advocating a win/lose strategy when clashing with others, Jesus taught that it was more godly to pursue a lose/win solution—to actually lose so that others might win a knowledge of the Kingdom.

> Love your enemies, do good to those who hate you, bless those who curse you, pray for those who mistreat you. If someone strikes you on one cheek, turn to him the other also. If someone takes your cloak, do not stop him from taking your tunic. . . . But love your enemies, do good to them, and lend to them without expecting anything back. Then your reward will be great, and you will be sons of the Most High, because he is kind to the ungrateful and wicked. Be merciful, just as your Father is merciful. (Luke 6:27-29,35-36)

Ultimately, of course, this lose/win strategy is exactly the course of action Jesus took in going to the cross. Though

He could have called down twelve legions of angels to save Him from death (Matthew 26:53), Jesus humbled Himself, became sin for us, and lost at the cross so that we might win everlasting life.

When taken all together, the example and the teaching of Jesus clearly indicate how we should act in conflict situations. We are to be infinitely patient with each other. We are never to give up on a brother or sister, but instead must quickly forgive and be reconciled. Even when we are treated in unloving ways, we have a duty to return good for evil, blessing for cursing. If in the end someone must lose, unless truth itself is at stake we must be willing to surrender rather than force defeat on someone else. That is the win/win strategy. More importantly, that is the nature of Christ.

BACK TO THE SCORPION

What is your nature? What creature do you become when faced with conflict in the Church? Do you, when your back is to the wall, find yourself in a fight or flight, win-or-lose mindset? Do you sting first, only to discover later that you have harmed yourself as much as your victim?

Like the scorpion, we can excuse our behavior with a shrug of the shoulders—"It's my nature to sting." For too long, Christians have justified their caustic behavior with the words, "That's just the way I am." Perhaps that is the problem! Perhaps what God's people need today is less excuse and more repentance.

God is in the people-changing business. He wants to take our nature and change it into His nature. By His power, He can take even a scorpion and transform it into His own image.

But change is easier to talk about than to accomplish. Unless God performs some overnight wonder on us, we face the sad reality that our natures seem cast in concrete. Though God has promised His help, He will not do *for* us what He can best do *with* us.

How do we cooperate with God in changing our nature? Unfortunately, there is no magic prescription: "Drink this and your troubles will be over. Three teaspoons each morning and you will become a carefronter for the whole day."

Yet there are some sane, simple measures we can implement to incorporate more of the nature of Jesus. Especially in the area of conflict, a few simple rules can keep us in a win/win mode. These rules are not designed to help you avoid conflict. They instead help you make conflict something growthful and beneficial. The key to Christlike conflict is not escape. It is learning to *fight fairly.*

DISCUSSION, REFLECTION, AND ACTION

Chapter Discussion

1. Briefly describe for the group one conflict you encountered during the past week and how you handled it. Did you do what the "Conflict Styles Inventory" suggested you would do?

2. On page 149, the authors say that there is a scorpion in each of us. Do you agree or disagree? Why?

3. In a power struggle with someone, how is it possible to "win the battle, yet lose the war"? Explain from your own experience, if you can.

4. How can the win/win conflict style promote relationships rather than destroy them?

5. a. On page 154, the authors state that Jesus was committed to winning people rather than arguments. Do you
   agree with this statement? Why or why not?
   b. If you agree, how can your group put this principle into
   practice? Think of some specific issues you are facing
   as a group.

6. Can you subscribe to the idea that it is better to lose an
argument than to win? Why or why not?

Optional: Do you think a scorpion can really change his
nature? If so, how is this possible? If not, why not?

Personal Bible Search
1. Read John 8:1-11.
   a. Describe the dilemma in which the Pharisees placed
   Jesus. (What two losing alternatives did you they think
   they were giving Him?)
   b. How did Jesus maintain His win/win stance?

2. Read Luke 6:27-31.
   a. Which of these commands is most difficult for you?
   Why do you think this is so hard?
   b. Is it realistic to think that a Christian can live this kind of
   win/win lifestyle? Why or why not?

3. Read Romans 14:19-21.
   a. What does it take to maintain peace?
   b. What principle should determine whether we do
   something that is debatable among Christians?
   c. Have you ever seen someone give up his rights for the
   sake of peace? Have you ever seen someone stand up
   for his rights and lose the real war? Describe those
   experiences.

Personal Reflection and Action

1. a. In what circumstances are you most prone to try a win/lose strategy of conflict?

   b. What situations make it hardest for you to maintain a win/win attitude?

2. Does this saying ring true to you: "It's not whether you win or lose but how you play the game"? Why or why not?

3. For the next seven days, ask God to keep you alert for conflicts and empower you to choose a win/win strategy of loving enemies, turning the cheek, etc. When you encounter conflicts, try to remember to ask God again. Draw on His grace to choose the win/win approach.

CHAPTER ELEVEN

The Church in the Ring

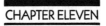

A number of years ago a group of family therapists in California tried to find a workable method for helping families resolve differences. Experience had taught them that conflict could not be removed from family situations. But wasn't there a way for couples to fight without ending up in divorce court? They set out to discover rules for fighting fair with people you love.

Believe it or not they actually developed a "Fight Clinic" with the avowed purpose of teaching couples the fine art of marital combat. You may be thinking, "Anything can happen in California!" But if you read Bach and Wyden's book *The Intimate Enemy,* much of their thinking rings true.[1]

People are bound to have differences—even people who love each other deeply. In fact, the only people without relationship difficulties are in cemeteries, although dying seems a rather drastic prescription for evading conflict.

The real question facing each of us is not *whether* we will have conflict but *how* it should be handled. Conflict is an inescapable part of existence, the reverse side of the coin we call relationship. Because conflict is inevitable, wisdom dictates that we learn to fight with decency and a sense of fair play. After all, even *boxing* has its "Queensbury Rules."

How we handle conflict sets limits on the degree of intimacy we achieve in our relationships. Relationships are built of material such as trust, mutual respect, and love. If we see conflict as a time when we suspend the normal rules of relationship—as a time when we can justifiably treat others *without* trust, respect, and love—the foundation of relationship crumbles. Even during the fight, there must be certain constraints which remind us that our opponent is also someone we love.

We have adapted Bach and Wyden's "fighting fair" techniques to the Church. Principles true for conflict in marriages turn out to be legitimate for conflict in local congregations. In fact, the Bible provides a wealth of illustrative material that underscores the importance and validity of these common-sense guidelines.

Here are seven rules for fighting in the Church, accompanied by the commentary of two author/preachers still learning about fighting fair. For the Church ever to conflict in a way that enhances rather than destroys intimacy, individual Christians must learn to observe these rules. You may want to: (1) memorize the rules and repeat them to yourself daily; or (2) tear out this chapter and carry it with you *at all times*; or (3) tattoo these maxims on your forearm for easy reference during times of conflict!

RULE #1. THOU SHALT NOT LOSE CONTROL.

One of the New Testament's most refreshing passages is Paul's permission for the Ephesians to "be angry" (Ephesians 4:26). But before we start practicing what Paul preached in this scripture, we had better read the rest of the verse. "Be angry, but don't sin." While not necessarily a sin, anger certainly can lead to sin. Anger's great temptation has to do with who will be in control: you or your emotions.

Anger is an ape that makes monkeys of us all. Its beguiling ways lure us into surrendering reason, restraint and respect. No one ever entirely masters his wrath.

But contrary to popular opinion, anger is not the same as loss of control. Far from it. When Paul states, "Be angry, but don't sin," he teaches that brothers and sisters can feel the emotion of anger without necessarily abdicating control to that emotion. It's when our anger persuades us to give free rein to our passions that sin creeps into conflicts.

This chapter is based on the premise that you can maintain sufficient self-control in a conflict situation to implement the rules for fair fighting. Yet anger can undermine this foundation. It can remove us from the driver's seat and usurp the steering wheel for itself. And when anger drives, your church is headed for the ditch.

That is why we must do whatever is necessary to keep respect and reason firmly in control during disagreements. A number of techniques can help us do this during conflict. Two of the most beneficial follow:

1. *Take your emotional temperature.* Stop (mentally) every few minutes to monitor your emotional state. Are you getting hotter? Being aware of your own emotions is the first step to keeping calm.
2. *Keep your volume down.* There seems to be a direct correlation between anger and voice level. In fact, an effective means of maintaining emotional calm is to concentrate on speaking more softly as the conflict progresses. (This has the added benefit of driving your opponent crazy!)

At times, however, maintaining control might only be possible by postponing a dispute until our emotions can be harnessed and disciplined. In some situations we are simply too angry to fight in a manner that would please Jesus. When these situations arise, we must use the last shred of control to remove ourselves from the situation before someone says something that all will regret.

So call a time out and share your fear of losing control. Walk around the block. Count to ten. Ask for a rain check. Do whatever it takes to keep a small spark from setting the whole forest on fire.

A doctor once asked an octogenarian how he had maintained such good health. The man answered, "Well, when my wife and I married, we agreed that if we couldn't resolve a difference, one of us would take a walk. I've done a lot of walking in all these years."

An expression of anger can be either a calm, honest statement of emotion or a broadside with every cannon you have on the ship. One way is beneficial. The other way is disastrous. The one is anger *under* control. The other is anger *in* control.

So learn to control yourself even in anger. By doing so you win the appreciation and respect of your brothers and sisters. And you prime the pump for better relationships once the conflict has passed. When I don't have to fear your wrath, I am free to cherish your friendship.

RULE #2. THOU SHALT NOT BRING UP THE PAST.

There is a sack I carry around,
It sits upon my shoulder.
Whenever I feel angry or mad
I put it in this holder.

Resentment goes in as well as hate,
Bitterness, heartbreak and blues.

If ever you choose to argue with me
You'll likely go into it too.

That sack is strong, it carries a lot.
But when it's full, some morning
I'll dump that sack upon your head
Without the slightest warning.[2]

One of the hardest lessons to learn about conflict is the wisdom of staying in the present when we clash. "Each day has enough trouble of its own" (Matthew 6:34) without bringing up arguments that separated us in the past.

But oh! How we love to reach into our sacks and bring back old business. Each new slight reminds us of the last time this brother or sister crossed swords with us. Something is eminently satisfying about making each new conflict an opportunity to refight past battles.

Ultimately, of course, such a strategy keeps us mired in yesterday's mud. We are not free to deal with present problems; the ghosts of bygone disputes still haunt us. Nothing escalates a conflict quite as effectively as bringing up the past. While a single issue has within it the hope of resolution, importing twenty-five old issues destroys any chance of settling matters quickly.

When Paul states, "Do not let the sun go down while you are still angry" (Ephesians 4:26), he intends for Christians to deal with conflicts as quickly as possible. But he also teaches us not to carry anger over into the future. What point is there in settling a conflict before the sun sets if bitterness over the conflict is still there when the sun rises again?

Deal with today's difficulties today. Refuse to carry disputes into tomorrow. Get rid of the sack on your shoulder. It will help us not to bring up the past if we will remember the following:

1. *Stick with one issue.* Don't bring up other conflicts, no matter how related they may seem to be. And don't allow others to do so. Constantly steer the discussion back to the issue at hand.
2. *Keep the emotion appropriate to the issue.* If you find yourself investing far more emotion in an issue than it reasonably deserves, that may be a good indication that old business is creeping into the conflict. You don't kill flies with shotguns. Nor should you become homicidal over the color of the new carpet for the auditorium.

A fellowship can stand the occasional flare-ups that are part of shared lives. It *cannot* stand the bitterness and resentment injected into those flare-ups by bringing up every hurt from the past. If we want fellowship after the fight is over, we must not allow the past to color the present.

RULE #3. THOU SHALT GIVE POSITIVE STROKES FIRST.

Before we can constructively discuss our differences, it is vital that we begin with a statement of appreciation. Taking a few moments to affirm our love and respect for the person with whom we differ sets the stage for Christlike conflict. After all, this person is not the enemy but part of Christ's body. It is important to recognize that fact.

Some people view giving positive strokes as just a namby-pamby, manipulative technique. No doubt for some people positive stroking is just a technique employed for self-serving reasons. Nevertheless, even in conflict we have a duty to "encourage one another and build each other up" (1 Thessalonians 5:11) and to "be kind and compassionate to one another" (Ephesians 4:32). If you sow kindness at the start of a disagreement, you will more likely reap a friend when the conflict is done.

Have you read 1 Corinthians lately? If you or I had written the book, our introduction might have read like this: "Dear Jerks. I've had it with you. How dare you call your-selves Christians?"

There were divisions in the Corinthian church: Christian took Christian to court; gross and blatant immorality was a subject for jokes; Paul's authority was challenged; the Lord's Supper became a drunken farce; believers boasted of their own spiritual gifts and disdained the gifts of others.

But please note how Paul begins that letter:

> To the church of God in Corinth, to those sanctified . . . and called to be holy. . . . I always thank God for you because of his grace given you in Christ Jesus. . . . He will keep you strong to the end, so that you will be blameless on the day of our Lord Jesus Christ.
>
> (1 Corinthians 1:2,4,8)

Paul is about to take them to task for the serious problems they brought on the Church. But he *begins* by giving *positive strokes first.* He affirms his commitment to them first. He assures them from the first that they are still his brothers and he is still their father in the faith.

When confronting conflict in the Church, Christians ought to follow Paul's example. The next time you find yourself at odds with another Christian, try starting out like this: "I know that you love God as much as I do and that you want what is best for His work. We seem to be on different sides of this issue and that concerns me because I respect your views. Tell me again what you are thinking and help me to see things from your perspective."

Differences must and should be discussed among Christians. But such discussions lead to deeper relationships only if they are framed within a context of our shared commitment, mutual respect, and optimistic faith in each another. When we take a moment to affirm what we appreciate about each other, we are much more likely to discuss lovingly those points on which we differ.

RULE #4. THOU SHALT FIX THE PROBLEM, NOT THE BLAME.

Whose fault is it when things go wrong? It seems almost instinctive for humans to evade personal responsibility for problems and to seek a luckless scapegoat to lay their faults upon.

Do you remember how the first couple acted when God reproached them for eating the fruit? Adam promptly blamed Eve for his transgression: "The woman you put here with me—she gave me some fruit from the tree, and I ate it" (Genesis 3:12). "Lord," Adam appears to say, "I was just an innocent bystander. Eve was the one who picked the fruit and forced me to eat it." Adam even seemed to attempt to lay some of the blame on God. After all, Eve was God's idea, not Adam's.

The text doesn't indicate how Eve felt about this. It goes without saying that Adam probably slept on the couch that night! At that moment, however, Eve was similarly busy looking around for someone else to take responsibility for her actions. She faulted Satan. "The serpent deceived me, and I ate" (Genesis 3:13). Whereas Adam protested his innocence, Eve pleaded helplessness in the face of Satan's lying ways. In reality, all of them shared the burden of guilt. God punished each one of them.

In all the millennia since then, human beings have not changed much. When problems arise we still cast about for someone to pin the blame on, as if *we* had no part in creating the problem, as if *we* were not responsible for some measure of the difficulty. The truth is that in most conflict situations, each of us contributes to the problem to one degree or another. In most human interaction, there is really no such thing as an innocent party.

When will we learn to fix the problem, not the blame? Blaming others may make us feel better, but it rarely solves our difficulties. It circumvents personal responsibility at the expense of our brothers and sisters. It promotes defensiveness rather than problem solving. If all the time, energy, and thought that goes into finding a scapegoat were spent on finding a solution, what a difference it could make!

So when you find yourself in a critical situation and your inclination is to find the nearest scapegoat, try the following instead:

1. *Determine to confess rather than blame.* Focus on your own faults. Concentrate on the way you have contributed to the problem and determine to make it right. Take the beam out of your own eye before looking for the speck in your brother's.
2. *Decide to protect rather than expose.* Help your brother save face instead of stripping him naked in front of others. Embarrassing someone (as blaming often tends to do) may help you win the argument, but it won't do much for relationships.
3. *Focus on solutions rather than scapegoats.* Keep asking the question, "What can we do to make this right?" instead of demanding, "Who is responsible for causing this to go wrong?"

As with all conflicts we must remember that there will always be a next time. When the next conflict comes, we may catch the blame and need a little kindness—"In the same way you judge others, you will be judged, and with the measure you use, it will be measured to you" (Matthew 7:2).

RULE #5. THOU SHALT NOT MIND-READ.

Jesus could read minds. Remember when the Pharisees doubted something Jesus said? "Immediately Jesus knew in his spirit that this was what they were thinking in their hearts" (Mark 2:8). That is an enviable ability.

Jesus, however, had many abilities not shared by His disciples. He walked on water, but few of us would try the same.

So why do we insist on reading each other's minds? What conceit allows us to believe we can know the thoughts of another? "I know what you're thinking!" "I know what you will say before you even say it." "I can read you like a book."

Is that really true? Every human being deserves the courtesy of being heard, especially a brother or sister. Yet how often do we presume to know another person's heart? We can barely discern our own motives, much less the purposes of others.

The single most important tool we can bring to conflict is a listening ear. True listening is more than that period of time during which I let you babble while I formulate my next statement. Listening is respect fleshed out. It communicates our regard for others, that we are more interested in finding truth than in making points.

Listening does not imply that we necessarily agree. To listen is not to capitulate. It is, however, to grant others the same respect you want them to grant you. How can we ask someone to consider our side of an issue if we are not willing to do the same for them?

For a fight to resolve into intimacy instead of alienation, each person in the conflict must be fully heard and truly understood. Neither bears nor Christians appreciate being backed into corners. When in our eagerness to win the argument we fail to listen respectfully to each other, we may well carry the point, but we risk losing a brother or sister. When we listen carefully, however, we set the stage for deeper relationships, no matter the outcome of a particular disagreement.

Solomon said, "He who answers before listening—that is his folly and his shame" (Proverbs 18:13). James admonishes us to take listening seriously when he states, "My dear brothers, take note of this: Everyone should be quick to listen, [and] slow to speak" (James 1:19). To accomplish this in conflicts, each of us should be careful to do the following:

1. *Give others a chance to talk.* If we dominate the conversation, it is certain that we are not hearing what others are saying. You cannot talk and listen at the same time. Make a conscious effort to close your mouth and open your ears.

2. *Concentrate on what is said.* Too often, our silence is used to organize what we will say next rather than as an opportunity for learning from the other person. Listening involves more than letting someone else speak—it is a commitment to think about what he says.

3. *Do an occasional listening check.* Take the time to summarize what the other person is saying. This not only allows you to determine whether you are hearing accurately but communicates that you are committed to understanding the other person's position.

RULE #6. THOU SHALT NOT LABEL.

The story is told of three baseball umpires who were discussing their philosophies of officiating at the plate. The first umpire stated firmly, "Some are balls and some are strikes, but I call 'em like I *see* 'em." The second umpire spoke just as firmly, "Some are balls and some are strikes, but I call 'em like they *are*." The third umpire smiled sagely and said, "Some are balls and some are strikes, but they ain't *nothing* till I call 'em."

Some Christians act like spiritual umpires, labeling brothers and sisters quite as casually as they would call strikes and balls.

"You liberal!"

"You stick-in-the-mud conservative!"

"Heretic!"

"Hypocrite!"

"Pharisee!"

"Publican!"

How easily labels come to our lips in the heat of battle. Have you noticed that when we run out of logic, we quickly resort to names? Especially when one is caught in a win/lose mode, labeling becomes an attractive weapon always within reach.

The Pharisees were masters of the well-placed label. An entire class of society they dismissed with the contemptuous label "tax collectors and sinners" (Luke 5:30, 7:39). Those who believed in Jesus they derided as a "mob that knows nothing of the law" (John 7:49). But it was for Jesus Himself that they reserved some of their most vicious labels. They called Him "a glutton and a drunkard" (Matthew 11:19). They accused Him of being "demon-possessed and raving mad" (John 10:20). Even after His death, the Pharisees referred to Him as "that deceiver" (Matthew 27:63).

The more frustrated the Pharisees became with Jesus, the more likely they were to call Him names. As Jesus' popularity grew, so did the list of labels applied to Him by the religious leaders. When they could no longer answer His logic, they chose to malign His character. At times, we must confess, we use the same strategy with our brothers and sisters.

Of course, the Church must at times deal with true heretics and deceivers. But such labels must be used only after the most serious consideration. In baseball, calling a strike a ball has little ultimate importance. But "calling it wrong" in the Church has immense consequences. Souls are at stake. Unfortunately, when labels fly in the Church, they are used more often to win arguments than to alert the Church to real dangers.

If we can avoid name-calling in the heat of conflict, the chances are much better for healing relationships when the conflict has ended. Labels are uniquely difficult to forget. Once you place a label on me, you hand me your evaluation of my whole character. It is difficult indeed to mend fences with someone whose language has left little doubt about his low estimation of my heart.

RULE #7. THOU SHALT NOT HIT BELOW THE BELT.

Each of us has vulnerable points, tender and sensitive spots on our psyches that can rarely survive a direct hit. It may be a son who has gone astray or a past indiscretion. Perhaps it is a failed business venture, a hurting marriage, or just an episode of bad judgment. Whatever your tender spot, it is your Achilles heel, your glass jaw.

In the course of time, we learn each other's vulnerabilities. With such knowledge, however, comes grave responsibility. "Knowledge is power," someone has said, and certainly that is true in conflict. Having mapped a fellow believer's hurts, we have the capacity to deliver a knockout blow. Just one punch, just one verbal uppercut, and we can reduce an opponent to impotence no matter what the real issue.

Two men were arguing over the teenage curriculum in an education committee meeting. One of the men had experienced real difficulties raising his daughter. The girl had come out right in the end, but not until after years of heartache and pain. As the disagreement between these brothers became more heated, the other finally stated, "With as much trouble as you had with your daughter, how can you know what is best for our teenagers?"

Guess who won this battle? It didn't matter that the one man may have learned some valuable lessons from his experience. Nor did it matter that his opponent was too young to have raised teenage children of his own. All that mattered was that one delivered a knockout blow, exploiting a point of vulnerability and reducing a brother to embarrassed and angry silence.

Hitting below the belt is never a fair tactic. The end never justifies resorting to this means. No matter what the issue, some things are so sensitive, so hurtful, that using them is tantamount to purposely breaking arms, legs, or necks for a win at any cost. We must not destroy in our eagerness to defend.

More of us need to cry "Foul!" when such a blow is delivered. Christians are not to be held eternally guilty for having hurts in their past. True guilt falls on the one who takes advantage of those hurts simply to win an argument. It is the act of hitting below the belt which is reprehensible, not the fact that the opposition has something below the belt to hit!

Many leaders in the early Church had much to be

ashamed of in their past. They too had their vulnerable points. Peter deserted and denied Jesus. Paul had persecuted the Church. John Mark (the author of the second gospel) had quit Paul and Barnabas on the first missionary journey. John, the apostle of love, had once wanted to call down fire to consume an entire village. What if the early Church had constantly reminded them of their pasts? Could they have turned the world upside down while their brothers and sisters were busy turning them inside out? Great mistakes did not disqualify these men from great service. And to the early Church's credit, these men were allowed to minister without fear of being walloped on these issues by their own brothers and sisters.

Hitting below the belt is the win/lose philosophy at its destructive worst. Where does it leave you when the fight is over? We may forgive someone who has opened old wounds, but we'll probably never trust him again. We may worship with him, but we'll have difficulty relating to him. He may still be a brother, but how can we ever call him friend?

If we want to survive conflict with the hope of deeper fellowship, we must protect each other from blows which can cripple and maim.

THE CHURCH IN THE RING

Turn on the TV any Saturday night and you're bound to be assaulted by *All Star Wrestling*. Mountainous men and virile women pretend to beat each other to a pulp while a helpless referee strives vainly to bring order to chaos.

The referee may be the most interesting participant. Have you ever figured out why he is there? By definition professional wrestling is a no-holds-barred, throw-away-the-rule-book, let's-have-a-brawl activity. The average spectator does not come to see a cleanly-fought match. He wants all the dirty-punching, below-the-belt action he can get.

That, of course, is why the referee is present. Breaking the rules of fair fighting wouldn't be any fun if someone were not around whose job it was to enforce the rules. He at least tries to keep things clean; in this situation he is doomed to fail.

Whether in the ring or in the pew, we need rules for fighting fair which must be observed if clean, aboveboard, honorable conflict is to occur. During conflict, the only thing which distinguishes the Church from a wrestling match is our desire to see those rules of fair fighting obeyed.

Unfortunately, the Church does not have referees who make us fight cleanly. No men in striped shirts hover around our conflicts. Rarely does any outside force make us adhere to the rules and call "Foul!" when we fail to observe them.

The only referees we have are ourselves. We must play both combatant and umpire. We not only strike the blows; we must judge whether we deliver those blows in love, in a way helpful for building others up. If we choose to throw the rules away, no one will step in to blow a whistle or send us back to our corners. We have absolute freedom to ignore the guidelines and beat one another to a bloody pulp.

But there is no victory in that. To stand over the broken remains of a brother or sister while gloating over the successful defense of our position is an empty triumph at best.

Real victory can come only when we respect one another sufficiently to observe the rules and fight fairly. Only at the end of a cleanly-fought contest can we come to the center of the ring and embrace one another. Each can know that even in the heat of battle, mutual love and respect prevented us from using tactics and techniques that might cause irreparable damage to the spiritual health of our opponent.

And who knows? In the course of the conflict we may even learn something about each other that deepens our respect, strengthens our appreciation, and forges a bond that can blossom into a precious fellowship.

DISCUSSION, REFLECTION, AND ACTION

Chapter Discussion

1. a. What happened during the past week when you encountered conflicts?
   b. Were you able to choose a win/win strategy? If so, what was the result? If not, what do you think prevented you?

2. The authors say, "People are bound to have differences—even people who love each other deeply." Is this valid in your experience? How, or how not?

3. a. Review the seven rules for fighting fair. Which do you think would be most helpful in your own fights? Why?
   b. Which of the rules did you find most surprising? Why do you think this happened?
   c. Do you disagree with any of the rules? If so, why?

4. a. Describe a situation in your life where you are at odds with someone else. (If such a situation exists within your group, address it.)
   b. How would the seven rules help you deal with it?

5. How might a church leader apply these rules to conflicts that arise within his church?

Personal Bible Search

1. Read 1 Peter 3:8-12.

    a. What does it involve to "live in harmony with one another"?

    b. To what have Christians been called?

    c. Which fighting-fair rule is closest to verse 9?

2. Read 1 John 3:7-10.

    a. How can we tell the difference between the person who is righteous and the one who is of the Devil? How can we distinguish between God's children and Satan's?

    b. John says that Jesus came "to destroy the devil's work" (3:8). Why should this fact motivate us to do everything we can to love each other?

    c. What does this passage have to do with the rules for fighting fair?

3. Read James 1:19-21.

    a. Which of the three things listed in verse 19 is hardest for you to do? Why do you think this is true?

    b. Why doesn't anger "bring about the righteous life that God desires"?

    c. Which fighting-fair rule sounds most like verse 19?

Personal Reflection and Action

1. a. Make a list of five areas of your life that really hurt when someone pokes at them with nagging or verbal attack.

    b. Share one or more of those with someone you trust, and pray about this issue together. Ask God to heal that spot so you won't lash out when prodded there.

2. Get together with someone and practice working through a situation that has been hard for you. Use the fighting-fair rules. (You could do this during your group meeting.)

3. Share any new insights you have gained about yourself.

CHAPTER TWELVE

Body Language

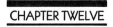

Be careful little hands what you do.
Be careful little hands what you do.
There's a Father up above
    looking down in tender love,
So be careful little hands what you do.

(Repeat about a thousand times, substituting for
"hands what you do" such things as "feet where you
go," "eyes what you see," "ears what you hear,"
"tongue what you say," etc.)

Simply because this is a child's song we mustn't assume
it contains a childish message. Life is full of pitfalls that
demand a watchful eye. The wise Christian pays attention to
the caution signs staked along life's road.

Relationships are like that. You'll be traveling along the
fellowship road without a care, only to hit a pothole or sharp
curve that lands you in the ditch. Some of those road hazards
take the form of conflicts and disagreements. Others are
more subtle, however, and have to do less with how relationships go wrong than with how they fail to go right at the
outset.

A few "be carefuls" apply to the latter type of hazard; these are rules for Christian relationships which if heeded help us to define and develop real relationships within God's Church.

When we speak of "real relationships" we mean fellowship characterized by the warmth, depth, and intimacy that Jesus Christ intended for His Church. The kind of relationship that meets our need to love and be loved. Fellowship based on agape rather than convenience—a tie that binds us so closely that the whole world can see we have been with Jesus.

If we are to develop that depth of relationship in our congregations, we must be careful about a few things.

BE CAREFUL WHERE YOU TALK

> Then, because so many people were coming and going that they did not even have a chance to eat, he said to them, "Come with me by yourselves to a quiet place and get some rest."
> So they went away by themselves in a boat to a solitary place.   (Mark 6:31-32)

Church buildings are perhaps the greatest impediment to Christian relationships the Church faces today. Those stained-glass sanctuaries have become expensive mausoleums in which many a relationship has been laid to rest.

We spend vast sums on beautiful foyers to draw in visitors and make them feel welcome. We build fellowship rooms equipped with the latest kitchen appliances and stackable furnishings so that Christians have a place to fraternize. The stated intent of all this construction is to provide space where members can greet and meet and eat. The unstated assumption is that the better our facilities, the more likely it is our people will spend time getting to know each other.

In reality, the opposite happens. Have you ever overheard this typical conversation taking place in church foyers all over the country?

"Hi, John. How are you doing?"
"Fine. How are you?"
"I'm fine, thank you. How's the wife?"
"She's fine. How is Sally?"
"She's doing just fine. Are the kids well?"
"They're fine. And yours?"
"Fine. They're fine. How do you like your new car?"
"Just fine. . . ."

Normally intelligent, expressive men and women revert to social clichés and surface banter when relating to brothers and sisters in the building. The edifice built to promote fellowship has become a breeding ground for shallow interaction. Are Christians just not interested in developing deeper, more meaningful fellowship, or might the problem be with the places where Christians talk?

A close correlation seems to exist between the erection of church buildings and the erosion of relationships in a church. We have no data to support this claim. We simply insist that *where* you talk limits the kinds of relationships you develop. Church buildings never encourage the type of fellowship that God intends for His children.

Foyers are loud places with lots of people. There isn't much privacy. People crowd shoulder to shoulder, hurrying to get in or hurrying to get out. You don't strike up intimate friendships in an environment like that. Moreover, fellowship rooms facilitate only the most surface kind of fellowship. At fellowship dinners we do a lot of eating but not much sharing. With the kids running around, the men fighting for seconds, and the women washing the silverware, there is no opportunity for working on real relationships. And the design of most auditoriums forces us to spend the majority of our time staring at the back of each other's head. It's hard to get friendly with a ponytail.

Loud, crowded, busy settings limit us to one kind of interaction—the kind we conduct at the top of our lungs and off the top of our heads. When people gather in such places, they are comfortable only with the surface and the safe. Our fellowshiping degenerates into polite superficiality and relationships stagnate. Until Christians move beyond their buildings and seek better environments for fostering intimacy, the Church is doomed to be a gathering of strangers.

The problem, of course, lies not in our church buildings so much as in the attitudes they cultivate. Buildings foster a dependency in congregations—once we build them we can't stay out of them. Most of our activities and get-togethers become captive to the facility. As we—like good stewards—attempt to maximize the use of our expensive properties, we spend most of our time with our brothers and sisters in an environment that stifles real relationships. Now we should be thankful that God provides His people with comfortable and convenient buildings in which to meet. But we should never view the building as the primary meeting place for Christians. When a church limits its meetings to its building, something good has gone rotten.

The Church of the first century used buildings for worship and teaching. In Jerusalem the church met at the Temple. In Ephesus the church used a lecture hall belonging to Tyrannus. But while Christians used such facilities, they did not restrict their interactions to these places.

The New Testament Church focused far more on the home than on the sanctuary. Many of those early congregations were small enough to meet exclusively in homes. It is important to notice, however, that no matter how large a congregation grew, it never met exclusively in a building.

The Jerusalem church numbered 3000 members from the day it was established. These believers constantly used the "Temple courts," assembling daily to enjoy public teaching and fellowship (Acts 2:42,46). However, they also met in homes—in small, intimate gatherings of brothers and sisters throughout the city (Acts 2:46). When they wanted to worship and listen to the apostles, they went to the Temple. When they wanted to share their lives and build real relationships, they went to a believer's house.

The home has always been the environment that molds individuals into a family unit. It is uniquely suited to developing the intimate relationships necessary for biological or spiritual families. The home is small and relatively quiet, private and relaxed. There in your living room, family pictures on the wall and cup of coffee in hand, you can share one-on-one those things central to your life as a Christian. Communication and rapport can flourish around a kitchen table. A far deeper fellowship can develop around a fireplace than in a foyer.

No wonder, then, we find such emphasis in the New Testament on hospitality and the home. The gospels indicate that Jesus used other people's houses extensively. Though often we find Him in the Temple or synagogue, more often He is sitting down to eat at a sinner's house or teaching His disciples in someone's living room. So fond was Jesus of the kitchen table that the Pharisees accused Him of being "a glutton and a drunkard" (Matthew 11:19). Yet He seemed to crave the quiet and informality that a house provided, especially for developing the apostles.

Jesus recognized that other places might be good for reaching the masses, but the home was uniquely suited to molding character.

This emphasis on hospitality carried over to the epistles. Twice the apostles commanded Christians to offer hospitality to one another (Romans 12:13, 1 Peter 4:9). Both of the chapters that detail qualifications for elders identify hospitality as a necessary characteristic (1 Timothy 3:2, Titus 1:8). The Church of the New Testament was a Church of the house. It was not the cathedral that shaped the character of the early Church but the warm and intimate contact afforded by open hearts and open homes.

The same ought to be true of the Church today. If we want to develop real relationships in local churches, we must balance how we use our buildings and our homes. When our purpose is to worship and educate, the building's value becomes evident. But when our purpose is to love and serve and share, nothing takes the place of a home dedicated to hospitality and to developing intimate relationships.

Unfortunately, many of us have forgotten the fine art of hospitality. The thought of opening our homes exhausts us. We are so busy, our lives so cluttered, that a free evening is hard to salvage. Working couples find it difficult to hurry home, clean the house, cook a meal, and then entertain guests. Overwhelmed, they decide to wait until life becomes less hectic before inviting anyone over. And they wait. And they wait.

Happily, you don't have to be Superman to be hospitable. The real problem lies not with our busy schedules but with our shallow notions of what genuine hospitality is about. Whoever said that a four-course meal was required? Buy a bucket of Kentucky Fried Chicken! Better yet, ask your guests to pick some up on the way over! It's not a good meal you are after, but good fellowship.

What does it matter if the house is a bit messy? Emily Post doesn't go to church where you do. And so what if you can only spare an hour or two? Better an hour spent with brothers and sisters than watching TV or mowing the lawn.

The point of hospitality is not to impress people but to get to know them. Your guests don't care what they eat—they're hungry for you. Don't get so hung up on the mechanics of hospitality that you forgo the purpose of it. If we want to deepen fellowship in the Church, we must be careful where we talk.

BE CAREFUL WHAT YOU TALK ABOUT

Let your conversation be always full of grace, seasoned with salt, so that you may know how to answer everyone.   (Colossians 4:6)

Some Christians wear their religion on their tongues. They sound like the *King James Version,* alerting everyone to their piety by the use of outdated English. Or perhaps you know someone who can't talk about grocery shopping without throwing in a "Hallelujah! Praise Jesus!" for good measure. Even a form of evangelical super-sincerity is going around: "I just really feel just so really thankful, really I just do."

Many of us find such language unnatural and pretentious. And we react by doing what most of us do so well—fleeing to the opposite extreme. Some Christians you could follow around for a month and never hear the faintest reference to God slip from their lips. We have grown uncomfortable talking about God and how He works in our lives. If it is true that what comes out of the mouth reflects what goes on in the heart, you have to wonder whether some of us still believe that God is alive and well and present with us today.

If we want to develop real relationships in the Church, we must pay attention to what we talk about. Spiritual relationships require talk about spiritual matters. Not every conversation between Christian brothers and sisters is necessarily "Christian." Just talking with Christians doesn't mean we are having a spiritual, upbuilding, encouraging dialogue leading to an intensified fellowship.

Places limit relationships primarily because they limit what we feel comfortable talking about. But, ultimately, real relationships depend not so much on setting as on *content*. It is discouraging that many Christians—no matter the setting—can rarely turn their conversation toward matters that expand their understanding and appreciation of each other. Even if we move back into our homes, we still might fail at significant relationships because we refuse to focus on spiritual issues.

How do our conversations with Christians differ from those with our nonChristian friends? If there is no difference in what we talk about, how can there be a difference in the kind of relationship we have? What makes Christian relationships distinctly Christian is not who we talk to so much as what we talk about. Christians talk about Christ and the Bible and the meaning of discipleship. If we never discuss those types of things, how can we claim to have Christian relationships?

It is important for brothers and sisters to talk about the weather and cars and football and the children. We need to share the nuts and bolts of each other's lives. Christians shouldn't feel compelled to furrow their brows and talk deeply every time they get together.

But we must not limit our conversations to the secular and the mundane. Jesus was not above discussing fishing or water or crops. He knew about people's lives and enjoyed sharing their daily concerns. But Jesus was not content to limit His conversations to that level. His knack was taking the ordinary and turning it toward the eternal. Fishing became a metaphor for evangelism, a conversation about water became a discussion of the Spirit, and a mustard seed became a symbol for faith.

What was true of Jesus must become true of His disciples today. If our relationships in the local body are to be profound, it is vital that we move just as easily as Jesus from the common to the sublime. Christians concerned about forming true fellowship must consciously work to avoid trivial pursuits in their conversations and to move on to matters of ultimate meaning.

We can learn, for instance, to pray naturally and easily with each other. We can share struggles and victories as we try to live pleasing lives before God. We can study the Bible together and feed each other's souls. We can spend time together serving the needy, reaching the lost, encouraging the weak, and loving the lonely. Out of these shared experiences is bound to grow a sense of community transcending anything we might find outside the Church.

Don't settle for foyer talk any longer. Strive to strike a balance in your conversation, sharing not only the surface of your life but the depths as well. If we want to build real relationships in the local church, we must be careful what we talk about.

BE CAREFUL WHO YOU TALK TO

When you give a luncheon or dinner, do not invite your friends, your brothers or relatives, or your rich neighbors; if you do, they may invite you back and so you will be repaid. But when you give a banquet, invite the poor, the crippled, the lame, the blind, and you will be blessed. Although they cannot repay you, you will be repaid at the resurrection of the righteous.

(Luke 14:12-14)

Some years ago, Tim struck up a friendship with a young man whose story highlights a common difficulty in the fellowship of the Church. Tim tells it: "One Sunday evening, just after the close of services, I was standing in the foyer enjoying a little foyer talk. Suddenly, the auditorium doors flew open, and out marched a college student with teeth and fists clenched. He was obviously upset.

"I chased after him to ask what was the problem. With real frustration and anger, he said, 'I get so mad when people won't talk to me!' The story that began to spill out slapped me in the face and called me to rethink my understanding of Christian fellowship.

"This young man (I'll call him Chris) was raised in a silent home. The TV took the place of human interaction, and Chris never learned some of the basics of relating to people. He had few friends growing up and even fewer now that he had come to college. Though highly intelligent, Chris was relationship dumb—he didn't know where to start when it came to people.

"Worship services were the only social activity he allowed himself. Lonely and afraid, he came on Sundays hoping to find a little human contact to break his growing sense of isolation. All week he prepared for that moment at the end of services when he could turn to the person seated next to him, extend a hand, and begin a conversation. For days he rehearsed what he should say and how the other person might respond and how he could reply in turn. He stored a dozen possible conversations in his head, hopeful that he could generate a few moments of fellowship.

"When Sunday morning arrived, Chris sat in the auditorium and waited for people to fill the seats around him. He agonized all service long, rehearsing the things he wanted to say and waiting for the closing prayer to come. At the 'Amen' he turned to the person next to him and said, 'Hello. I'm Chris' and prayed that this time something special might happen.

"Time after time, though, the people seated next to Chris had other things to do and other people to see. After exchanging greetings and a few pleasantries, they excused themselves to strike up conversations with people they knew better and liked more. When Chris charged out of the auditorium that particular evening, he had failed once again to connect with a brother, and was at the end of his rope."

Granted, Chris's problem was extreme. He was not the easiest person to talk to in that auditorium. He was awkward and nervous. He was unsure of himself. He didn't quite know what to say or how to say it. He was playing a game without knowing the rules. But it is clear that no one present that evening needed loving more than this young man. All he asked for was someone to talk to him and spend some time. All he got was an empty hello and a quick exit.

In short, Chris was not a YAVIS person. YAVIS is an acrostic standing for:

Y—Young
A—Attractive
V—Verbal
I—Intelligent
S—Social

We like this kind of people in the Church. We delight in people full of youth and energy. We enjoy well-groomed, fluent conversationalists. We appreciate the gifted and well-educated. We value the socially skilled. When they walk through our doors, we rush to make them feel at home, ushering them to the best seats and introducing them to the preacher. It flatters us when they want to join our fellowship.

But how does the Church deal with non-YAVIS people? What about those neither young nor attractive? How do the uneducated and unkempt fare? What do we do with the Chris's in our congregations?

One of the things that differentiates relationships in the Church from those in the world is the way Christians relate to non-YAVIS people. Any social group or civic organization eagerly welcomes beautiful people. To be different from the Kiwanis Club, however, we must respond with the same enthusiastic warmth to the not so beautiful. More to the point, we must redefine our understanding of where real beauty lies.

Christians have a responsibility to be careful who they talk to. We must be mindful not to choose relationships simply based on who meets our needs or measures up to our criteria. The intimacy to which God calls us in the Church must not depend on conversational ability or social acumen. Yet in too many of our churches, the YAVIS standard becomes the measure by which we evaluate brothers and sisters. Those weighed in this balance and found wanting may still be accepted into membership. Whether they are accepted into *fellowship* is another matter.

When you look at Christ, however, you find Him using another standard. Certainly He spent time with the YAVIS crowd. He rubbed elbows with the religious and political leaders. He enjoyed the hospitality of the rich and the socially prominent. He could meet with a Nicodemus and love a rich young ruler. But it was not those characteristics that mattered to Jesus. He weighed men and women on a different scale.

When you look more closely at His interactions, you find that He spent most of His time with the non-YAVIS masses of the day: the poor and outcast, the sinners and diseased. His closest companions were not drawn from the pages of the social register. They were fishermen and tax-collectors and revolutionaries. Jesus seemed more comfortable with prostitutes than with Pharisees. You don't have to follow our Lord very long to see that He valued broken hearts and repentant souls far more than social skills and stylish clothing.

As Jesus' disciples, we are responsible to look more deeply into people, to see beyond the thin veneer of education or economics or social development. We strike up relationships with each other not because we are alike or because it feels good but because we are committed to the same Lord. Rich or poor, young or old, chic or dowdy—such things become irrelevant in the face of our common need for a merciful Savior.

Remember—it was while we were still His enemies that Christ died for us. He didn't come to us because we were clean and fresh and attractive. He loved us when we were unlovely. How ungrateful for those so loved to turn up their noses at their fellow servants. Such behavior is always the pot calling the kettle black.

Christians can do better than that. We form relationships as much for what we can do for others as what they can do for us. We do not allow personal preferences or chemistry to determine our relationships—agape will do that. Though we should not apologize for enjoying the company of people who are easy to love, we must determine not to restrict our relationships to such people. More than a few non-YAVIS people sit in our congregations needing our time and attention as well.

God promises to reward us for reaching out to the

poor, the lame, and the blind. Often that reward is given at "the resurrection of the righteous." Sometimes, however, the reward comes more quickly.

Tim continues his story about Chris: "He and I began to meet regularly. We talked about listening and sharing—the basic building blocks of relationships. Most importantly, we spent time together and became friends ourselves. Chris knew that at least one person at church cared about him and enjoyed his company.

"What a change it made! Chris became more confident and less awkward. He met a Christian girl and started dating. He made friends with other college students in the congregation. Two years later, this once shy, withdrawn, hesitant young man was preaching the gospel on a mission trip to Thailand. Like a plant in the desert, all he needed was a bit of water to make him bloom."

People like Chris sit in the pews of every congregation in this country. They turn to us, asking for our time and attention. If Jesus were sitting next to them, we know exactly what He would do. When the Church is ready to develop Christlike relationships, we, like Jesus, will be careful who we talk to.

ON THE ROAD TO REAL RELATIONSHIPS

When Jesus commanded us to love one another, He never promised it would be easy. All kinds of hazards block the road to real relationships. Individualism, diversity, conflict—each provides a unique challenge to preserving a Christlike fellowship. But even before these issues arise, fundamental questions need answers. Our answers determine the kind of relationships the Church will build.

Will we open our homes to each other, unlocking an environment where relationships can grow, or will we be content with foyer fellowship and Sunday associations? Will we open our souls on issues which make our relationships distinctly Christian, or are we too comfortable with the surface and the safe? Will we open our hearts to those whose sole claim to our affection may be their desperate need for *agape* love, or will we, like the world, do for others only if they can do for us?

As we travel along the fellowship road, potholes are around every curve. If we pay attention to the caution signs, however—heeding some essential "be carefuls"—we can miss a few of the hazards and travel farther toward our destination than ever we have before.

> There's a Father up above
>> looking down in tender love,
> So be careful little hands what you do.

DISCUSSION, REFLECTION, AND ACTION

Chapter Discussion

1. Recall your last set of post-service chats at church. How many of them were like the dialogue on page 183? How many were substantially deeper?

2. What are some characteristics of places in which you find easiest to open up and get to know others?

3. Do you agree that people's homes are good places in which to build real relationships? Why or why not?

4. a. Would you describe your group as one that uses a lot of religious language, or one that goes to what the authors call "the opposite extreme" (page 187)? Why?

    b. Do the members of your group use a lot of religious language when apart from other Christians, or do you avoid it? Why?

5. a. How can you as a group develop ways of praying and sharing naturally with each other?
    b. How can you learn to talk naturally with others about God's role in your life?

6. Do you think non-YAVIS people have a hard time fitting into your group or attending your church? Why or why not?

Personal Bible Search
1. Read 1 Peter 4:8-10.
    a. Why does love cover a multitude of sins?
    b. Why is hospitality so important?
    c. Why is it necessary to tell people to offer hospitality without grumbling?
    d. What gifts do you have that enable you to serve others?

2. Read Hebrews 13:1-3.
    a. What do you think it means to love each other as brothers?
    b. What is the difference between a brother and a stranger?
    c. Why is it also important to entertain strangers?

3. Read Galatians 2:11-14.
    a. What do you think eating at separate tables would have eventually done to Jewish and Gentile Christians?
    b. What lessons does this offer to modern Christians?

Personal Reflection and Action
1. Brainstorm a list of ways for you to get to know others in

the group better. Now attempt one of these this week.

2. Find someone in your group who seems to have a gift for meeting and helping others. Spend some time talking with and watching that person to learn how you can become more hospitable.

3. Do you think you are more or less hospitable than your parents were? Why do you suppose this is so?

CHAPTER THIRTEEN

A Better Church Begins with Me

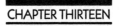

It sounded like the thing to do. With interest rates soaring, remodeling their home seemed the best direction to go. Building a new house would require the couple to go beyond their financial abilities. Yes, a sweat-equity remodeling job was the right decision for them.

John was a do-it-yourselfer. Marsha would try to stay out of the way. They threw themselves into the project: they removed old plaster, replaced appliances, framed new doors, and sanded floors. John was enjoying himself. Marsha was getting a headache. Days stretched into weeks and then months. At every step of the project, new problems arose. The first loan was quickly gone and the couple had to go even deeper in debt. John was determined to see things through. Marsha was considering suicide.

At last the project was completed. Finishing touches were applied, the last mess cleaned up, all the carpenters and plumbers and electricians banished from the house. John promised he would never go through such agony again. Someone heard Marsha say, "Now we can start building that garage!"

John and Marsha are not the only ones who have sung the "Remodeling Blues." Living in a house under construction is most people's idea of a nightmare. We admire people who attempt it—in the same way we admire people who hit themselves in the head with a hammer. Why would reasonable people willingly torture themselves by living in the middle of a remodeling project? Sawdust flying through the air, lumber stacked in bedrooms, cold drafts and late nights—few who have been through the experience once look forward to doing it again.

For brave souls who endure the agony, only a vision of the end product keeps them sane. Couples who lose sight of the goal are quick to call it quits.

Yet if the truth be known, each of us lives in a construction zone. To be a Christian is to be a house under construction. Discipleship is a continuing commitment to renovation and change. Christians recognize that the biggest room in anybody's life is the room for improvement. When improvement is the name of the game, remodeling is the only way to win.

What is true of the Christian individually is equally true of Christians collectively. The Church itself is a house under construction. Old attitudes and behaviors must be torn down, and new, more Christlike thinking erected in their place. Fresh perspectives must be painted over yesterday's traditions. Rooms adequate for the needs of the Church in times past must be enlarged and remodeled for the Church of the future.

While some of us approach the task with eagerness and vigor, others reach for the aspirin. Days stretch into weeks and months, and even the most enthusiastic remodelers begin to wonder if the process will ever end. Only a clear vision of the goal keeps us going. Only the sense that we are restoring this house to the dimensions intended by its original architect allows us to proceed with patience and determination.

Proceed we must, for God's House is looking ratty around the edges. The precious mortar which binds us together has deteriorated to the point that—in many congregations—the only thing holding us up is the weight of habit and obligation. When winds of controversy and conflict blow strong, the entire structure threatens to collapse. It is time for repairing God's Church so that once more we can be "knit together in love" (Colossians 2:2, NASB).

BUILDING A RELATIONSHIP CHURCH

How do we go about remodeling the Church along relationship lines? Some Christians point the finger at the Church, insisting that change can only come when *it* is willing to improve. Such an attitude lays the problem squarely on everybody else. "It is the leaders who are at fault." "It is our church hierarchy that needs to change." "It is all those uncommitted and unloving members who hold us back." Until *they* get their act together, goes the conventional wisdom, the Church can never hope to be what God intends.

A problem permeates this kind of thinking, however. If we are not careful, we end up believing "A better Church begins with *them.*" Though it is infinitely more comfortable to assert "they" are the problem, it is also infinitely more hopeless. If "they" are in fact the problem, there is next to nothing I can do to make a difference. I can feel frustrated and angry and hurt, but I do not have the power to change other people.

We find ourselves saying, in essence, that the Church cannot change until the Church changes—a wonderful piece of nonsense that keeps us forever mired in the problems of the present.

A far more hopeful position is the statement "A better church begins with *me.*" As I change, the Church will change. This perspective places the responsibility for transformation where it truly belongs—on the shoulders of every Christian. This attitude reflects an unbounded optimism about the ability of the individual to make a difference in the Church. Each member's efforts can gradually produce a congregation more loving, more kind, and more considerate of others. Instead of waiting around for someone else to straighten up, for someone else to do something, for someone else to make a difference, individual Christians take it upon themselves to be the catalyst for change so needed in the Church today.

If a better Church begins with a better me, all of us must consider some harsh realities. As soon as we stop blaming "them" for the Church's troubles and learn to see ourselves at the root of the problem, we must study ourselves in the mirror to discover the changes needed in our own lives. Self-analysis, while never easy, is the starting point for rejuvenated congregations.

If you have finished these pages without experiencing a profound *repentance,* we have failed to communicate the core of our concerns. Our ultimate purpose is neither to educate nor to expound. We write to convict. Our prayer is that the need for change will personally confront each one who reads this book. In years of struggling with this material, the authors never fail to be challenged by the same realization.

THE ROOM FOR IMPROVEMENT

When it comes to loving others, *we are not what we ought to be.* None of us is beyond the need for change. Rather than focus on the Church's illnesses, we would do well to first heal ourselves. Aspects of our personalities have not been remade into God's image. Our attitudes about relationships often smack more of the world than of the Christ. And each one of us does things in the heat of conflict that are more worthy of barbarian hordes than of Christians. May God forgive us. We are not what we ought to be.

In that confession, however, lies the seed from which a stronger Church will grow. Confucius said that the journey of a thousand miles begins with the first step. Though the Church has a long way to go before it becomes what God intended, that first step can only be taken by men and women convicted that they are not yet what God wants them to be. Repentant Christians are the best beginning for changed churches.

In reality, that change has already started. It doesn't take long to admit *we are not what we used to be.* However briefly we have walked with Christ, each of us can see changes which His Spirit has produced within us. The beauty of the Christian message is that while we are in the remodeling business, we do not pretend to be do-it-yourselfers. It is *Christ* at work within us, refurbishing our insides and smoothing out the rough edges.

If Christ is in you, you have witnessed some remarkable changes in yourself already. The gruffness you inherited from your father has mellowed into kindness and gentleness. The selfishness you inherited from Adam has changed into a genuine concern for others. The impatience you developed all on your own has melted into forbearance and acceptance. You are not the same person you were when you first met Jesus. Therein lies hope.

Of course, even these changes pale in comparison to what the future holds. *We are not what we're going to be.* Christ has something in mind for us that goes far beyond what we can ask or imagine. The One who has been working to transform us into God's image will continue to work inside us. We do not fear those changes—we welcome them! It is our desire to become more like Him that propels us into an uncertain future with eagerness and excitement. We cannot fear the results of remodeling so long as He is our architect and builder.

So let's be patient with each other—God's not through with us yet. The same process at work within each of us is also at work in our brothers and sisters. No, they are not what they ought to be. But neither are they what they used to be, or what God has in store for them in years to come. The same patience we ask others to show as God works in our lives we must extend to others as God works in them.

All of us are under construction; all of us still have our share of rough edges. As we strive to make the Church a relationship place, we cannot afford to criticize others for the same shortcomings we find in ourselves. Patience is the greatest tool of those who would change the Church. Neither Rome nor Christians can be built in a day. It took three long years for Jesus to work on the Twelve, and even then the task was not completed. If He can be so patient with them (and with us), we can afford to be patient with each other, recognizing that God is not yet through with any of us.

A BETTER CHURCH BEGINS WITH ME

Do we want a relationship Church? *A better Church begins with me.* I can begin to build relationships in my local congregation. There is no need for my church to implement a program or pass a proposition. I—one Christian who knows the importance of love—can look for people as hungry as I am for real fellowship and start loving them as Christ has loved me.

Do we want a more hospitable Church? *A better Church begins with me.* I must become more hospitable. Rather than bemoaning the lack of neighborliness among the Christians I know, I can quietly determine to open my home, share my table and give relationships a chance to develop. There is no need to wait for others to begin. Each one of us has the power to begin ourselves and make a small difference in the quality of the Church's fellowship.

Do we want a more accepting Church? *A better Church begins with me.* I must broaden the range of my friendships and learn to love those who need my love most. Why complain about what others fail to do? I can get busy being obedient to God myself. There is a Chris in my congregation just waiting for me to stop criticizing others and start accepting him. That's where real changes begin in the Church.

Nothing hinders us from building a relationship Church more than our own inertia. If God's House is to be remodeled into a relationship place, someone must have the courage to pick up a hammer and start working in his tiny corner of the Church. When one of us sets to work with a will, others will eagerly follow.

A better Church begins with me. And with you. And with all who take seriously the command to love one another. May God multiply such people throughout His Church. And may He use us to bring about a renovation in the Body of Christ that will show all the world that we are truly His disciples.

DISCUSSION, REFLECTION, AND ACTION

Chapter Discussion

1. How important to *you* is the goal of transforming your church into a place for committed, godly relationships? Explain.

2. On page 200, the authors say, "Discipleship is a continuing commitment to renovation and change." Do you agree or disagree? Why?

3. a. The authors claim that valuable change in your church has to begin with *you.* Give all the reasons why you might think this isn't so.
   b. Which arguments convince you? Why?

4. How do you feel about each of the following statements? (Are they accurate? Do they reassure or disturb you?) Why?
   ● We are not what we ought to be.
   ● We are not what we used to be.
   ● We are not what we're gonna be.
   ● Be patient with me. God's not through with me yet.

5. What can you as a group do to start making your church a "warmer place"?

Personal Bible Search

1. Read Genesis 13:5-9.
   a. What problem arose between Abram and Lot?
   b. Describe Abram's attitude in this conflict. Why was he able to have this attitude?
   c. What can you learn from this passage about how to respond to conflicts of interest?

2. Read Ephesians 4:25-32.
   a. Make a list of the instructions and statements in this passage that have to do with relationships.
   b. On what basis are we to forgive each other (verse 32)? Why is this important to keep in mind?
   c. Why is forgiveness so crucial to the life of a local church?

3. Read Matthew 18:21-35.
   a. In Jewish culture, the number 7 symbolized completeness and the total essence of something. What is Jesus' point in verses 21-22?
   b. What do you think is the chief point of the parable in verses 23-35?
   c. What does verse 35 have in common with Ephesians 4:32?

Personal Reflection and Action

1. a. What room in your spiritual "house" do you think God currently wants to concentrate on for improvement?
   b. What are you going to do about it? (Start with prayer.)

2. As a group and as an individual, will you make a prayerful commitment to make your church a better place where people who come will be *Among Friends*?

Conflict Styles Inventory

INSTRUCTIONS . . . PLEASE READ CAREFULLY.

Below are twelve scenarios you might encounter as an active member of your local church. For each situation, you are given five possible responses. Please imagine yourself in these situations (even better, remember a time when something very similar happened to you) and then study each of the possible responses carefully. Circle the letter of the response that you think would most closely describe your behavior in the scenario.

Fight the temptation to pick the most "Christian" response and honestly indicate how you normally would act. This is not a test. There are no right and wrong choices.

Choose only one response for each scenario.

Scenario One
Your two-year-old child is misbehaving during a worship service. You have "shushed" him or her several times. A woman in the next pew turns around to glare at you. You are angry and embarrassed. You would:

a. Increase your efforts to discipline the child.
b. Ignore the woman's look and do nothing different.
c. Spend the rest of the worship service in the nursery worrying that the woman will be upset with you.
d. Remove the child from the auditorium and pray that the woman will forget this unfortunate incident.
e. Take the child to the nursery and, later, speak with the woman about the struggle of teaching a child to behave in church.

Scenario Two

A member of the church you attend has been saying some things about you that are not favorable. When you learn of this, you are hurt and feel that you are being maligned. You would:

a. Go immediately to the person in an attempt to heal the rift between the two of you.
b. Just continue to be yourself so that the other person does not feel even worse toward you.
c. Try to give your side of the story to anyone who has heard the rumor.
d. Confront the gossiper and insist on an apology.
e. Avoid that person whenever possible.

Scenario Three

Your congregation has been looking for a new minister for some time. After examining several candidates, you are shocked to learn that the least desirable candidate (in your opinion) seems to have the strongest support. A congregational vote to determine your next minister will be held soon. You would:

a. Keep your doubts to yourself so as not to rock the boat.
b. Speak out clearly both about your reservations and

your resolve to fully support whomever the congregation invites.
c. Gather the names of people who feel as you do to show church leaders that the candidate does not have unanimous support.
d. Suggest to church leaders that more candidates should be interviewed before a decision is made.
e. Vote with the majority in spite of your doubts for the sake of good relations all around.

Scenario Four

Recently, a young man joined your church and began to attend your Sunday school class. He tends to dominate the discussion, interrupting others and making it difficult for the teacher to cover his material. Some long-time members of the class have stopped coming. You would:
a. Encourage the teacher to reprimand the man the next time he interrupts or dominates other class members.
b. Find another class to attend.
c. Invite the young man to your home for dinner and, after spending some time getting to know him, share your perceptions of his behavior.
d. Listen attentively to the young man when he speaks in class so that he feels appreciated and accepted.
e. Make some subtle comments in class about listening to others in hopes that the young man will take the hint.

Scenario Five

Your preacher has been making statements recently in his sermons that seem contrary to your understanding of the Bible. This bothers you greatly, although no one else in the congregation has voiced concern. You would:

a. Convince yourself that the preacher knows more about the Bible than you and say nothing.

b. Go to the Christian bookstore and buy a book on doctrine so that you can understand the issues better.

c. Decide that your relationship with the preacher is more important than your differences.

d. Voice your concerns to church leaders and other members of the congregation who should know what is happening.

e. Privately confront the preacher with your concerns and listen to his explanation.

Scenario Six

You have worked long and hard in an effective ministry of your church. Recently, several members of the church have voiced strong opposition to future plans for this ministry. They have not been active in this work, but nonetheless carry some weight with the leadership. You would:

a. Conclude that this "program" should not stand in the way of good relationships and mutual respect.

b. Decide that critics who are not doing the work are really not worth listening to.

c. Resign quietly from that particular ministry and find some other area in which to work.

d. Meet with those people, listen to their objections, and challenge them to support this good work.

e. Tone down your proposals for the coming year so that they do not seem so ambitious.

Scenario Seven

One of your Christian brothers or sisters is upset with you. He or she angrily confronts you after the worship service one Sunday and lets you know (in no uncertain terms) that you are in the wrong. You feel attacked and condemned. You would:

a. Suggest a time and a place better suited for resolving differences and indicate your willingness to meet.

b. Continue to apologize and request forgiveness until the other person calms down.

c. Admit that everyone makes mistakes, and apologize for "anything I might have done to upset you."

d. Get away as soon as possible.

e. Point out that he or she has also made his or her share of mistakes.

Scenario Eight

You have reason to believe that one of your Christian friends has a problem with alcohol. You care about this friend and want to help him or her before greater trouble develops. You would:

a. Talk to his or her friends and family about ways of getting this person into treatment.

b. Risk your friendship by confronting your friend about this problem.

c. Say nothing since you can't be of any help to this friend if he or she is mad at you.

d. Discuss your fears with the minister because he might know better what to do.

e. Decide that the matter is too personal and that someone closer to this individual should take responsibility.

Scenario Nine

You know a family in your church that has been very active and faithful. Recently, however, you have not seen this family at worship services. You are afraid that they may be losing their interest in religious matters. You would:

a. Promise yourself to ask them where they've been the next time they may show up at church.

b. Tell the minister that this family is not coming to worship, and that the congregation needs more hardhitting sermons on church attendance.

c. Want to call them, but decide not to for fear of intruding.

d. Call the family, invite them to dinner one evening, and bring up the subject over coffee and pie.

e. Make sure they are receiving the bulletin and other church literature as gentle reminders of the activities they used to enjoy.

Scenario Ten

The church you attend has decided to raise a rather large sum of money to remodel the auditorium. You think the money would be better spent feeding the hungry or supporting a missionary. You would:

a. Give a little money to the effort just so you could say that you participated.

b. Send your money to what you consider a more worthy cause.

c. Express yourself strongly to church leaders, committing to respect their motives even if you cannot agree with their ultimate decision.

d. Decide that you shouldn't jeopardize relationships over a little carpet and paint.

e. Withhold your contributions for a period of time.

Scenario Eleven

A new evangelism program is being started in your congregation. One of the leaders of this program calls to invite you to hold an evangelistic Bible study in your home. Although you believe in personal evangelism, the thought of sharing your faith with strangers scares you to death. You would:

    a. Confess that evangelism scares you, and ask if there are other ways to support this ministry.

    b. Support the effort by attending the training sessions, but look for a good opportunity to back out.

    c. Promise to go to the organizational meeting before making up your mind one way or the other.

    d. Tell him that not everyone is gifted to share his or her faith with strangers.

    e. Tell him you will think about it and hope that he forgets having asked you.

Scenario Twelve

You are working on a committee to plan a benevolence program for the church. Though the members of the committee feel strongly about providing food, clothing, and other types of assistance to those in need, they are divided over how that should be accomplished. You are frustrated that things are moving so slowly. You would:

    a. Work out a compromise plan so that the committee can get on with its work.

    b. Keep on discussing the matter, listening carefully to others' ideas, even though more time is required.

    c. Use all the influence you have in the committee to get them to adopt the proposed plan.

    d. Wish silently that someone would decide something.

    e. Decide not to complicate matters and agree to whatever the other members think is best.

DETERMINING YOUR CONFLICT STYLES

Order and Range of Style Preferences

1. In Box 1, circle the same letter for each choice that you circled in your inventory. (This designates the "conflict

style" you chose for each scenario.)

2. Add the number of scenarios in which you used a particular conflict style and enter the total in the row labeled "Scores."

Scenarios	Your Response Choices				
#1	E	C	D	B	A
#2	A	B	E	D	C
#3	B	E	A	C	D
#4	C	D	B	A	E
#5	E	C	A	D	B
#6	D	A	C	B	E
#7	A	B	D	E	C
#8	B	C	E	A	D
#9	D	E	C	B	A
#10	C	D	A	E	B
#11	A	B	E	D	C
#12	B	E	D	C	A
SCORES					
CONFLICT STYLES	Carefront	Comply	Avoid	Compete	Compromise

Box 1

ORDER OF YOUR STYLE PREFERENCES		
Choice	Style	Score
1st		
2nd		
3rd		
4th		
5th		

Box 2

3. In Box 2, list your conflict styles and scores in descending order of response frequency.

Box 2 now provides you with two important insights into your conflict behavior, and says something about your general philosophy and orientation toward conflict.

You now have a rough rank ordering of your conflict styles preferences. The style chosen most frequently is the style you are probably most comfortable with in conflict situations. You will tend to enter most conflict situations with this preferred style. The next style chosen would then constitute your "fall back" style if the first proves to be ineffective.

You also have an indication of the range of styles you are able or willing to utilize. If you selected only one or two styles with any frequency, you may have a limited range of conflict management behaviors. If your selection of styles was more evenly balanced, you evidence a wider range of conflict management styles.

This survey is an adaptation of the "Conflict Styles Survey" that appears in Norman Shawchuck's *How to Manage Conflict in the Church* (Spiritual Growth Resources, 1983). Adaptation completed with author's permission.

*

ENDNOTES

CHAPTER 1: THE CHURCH IN CRISIS

1. Francis Schaeffer, speaking at a meeting of ministers and church leaders in Wheaton, Illinois, in 1977. Dr. Schaeffer was in Chicago to promote his film series "How Should We Then Live." This statement is typical of Schaeffer's strong belief in the need for the church to be a community of believers, not just a repository of doctrine. Compare two more of Schaeffer's quotes, taken from *The Church at the End of the 20th Century* (Downers Grove, Ill.: InterVarsity Press, 1970, pages 72-74.)

"The church will not stand in our generation, the church will not be a striking force in our generation unless it keeps a proper balance between form and freedom in regard to the polity of the church, unless it keeps the strength of the Christian dogmas and at the same time produces communities with beauty as well as truth. . . .

"Does the church have a future in our generation? Only if it shows not only the form of Scripture at the point of proper polity, but also the form of Scripture at the point of proper community. If it does not show both together, we have missed the whole lot. One stands along with the other."

CHAPTER 2: THE URGE TO MERGE

1. Rene Spitz, "Hospitalism: An Inquiry into the Genesis of Psychiatric Conditions in Early Childhood," *Psychoanalytic Study of the Child*, vol. 1 (1945), pages 53-74.
2. *The Playboy Report on American Men*, poll conducted by Lewis Harris and Associates, analysis and interpretation by William Simon and Patricia Y. Miller (Chicago: Playboy, 1979).

CHAPTER 3: GOD'S RELATIONSHIP PLACE

1. Gary Portnoy and Judy Hart Angelo, "Theme From Cheers (Where Everybody Knows Your Name)" (Miami: CPP/Belwin, Inc., 1982).
2. *Theological Dictionary of the New Testament*, 10 Vols., Gerhard Kittel ed., Geoffrey W. Bromiley trans. (Grand Rapids: Wm. B. Eerdmans Publishing Company, 1965), vol. 3, page 797.
3. Kenneth Mitchell, *Theology News and Notes*, October 1978.
4. Bruce Larson and Keith Miller, *The Edge of Adventure* (Waco, Tex.: Word Books, 1974), page 156.

CHAPTER 4: WILL THE REAL CHRISTIAN PLEASE STAND?

1. The basic outline for this chapter is drawn from an appendix ("The Mark of the Christian") included in Francis Schaeffer's *The Church at the End of the 20th Century* (Downers Grove, Ill.: InterVarsity Press, 1970).
2. Francis A. Schaeffer, *The Church at the End of the 20th Century*, page 139.

CHAPTER 6: A DECLARATION OF DEPENDENCE

1. Paul Simon, "I Am a Rock," *Sounds of Silence*, 1965.
2. Alvin Toffler, *Future Shock* (New York: Bantam Books, 1971), page 78.
3. John Barth, *The Floating Opera* (Garden City, N.Y.: Doubleday and Company, Inc., 1967), page 7.
4. Gerald Hawthorn, *Word Biblical Commentary*, vol. 43: *Philippians* (Waco, Tex.: Word Books, 1985), page 63.
5. Karl Barth, *The Epistle to the Philippians*, J.W. Leitch, trans. (Richmond, Va.: John Knox Press, 1962).

CHAPTER 7: OF PEACOCKS, CRANES, AND CHRISTIANS

1. *Aesop's Fables* (Norwalk, Conn.: The Heritage Press, 1969), page 23.

CHAPTER 8: IF THIS IS PEACE, WHO NEEDS WAR?

1. H. Milman, *History of Latin Christianity*, 8 Vols. (New York: A.C. Armstrong & Son, 1903), vol. 4, page 251.
2. Will Durant, *The Story of Civilization*, vol. 4: *The Age of Faith* (New York: Simon and Schuster, 1950), page 784.
3. Bruce Felton and Mark Fowler, *Felton and Fowler's Best, Worst and Most Unusual* (New York: Gramercy Publishing Company, 1984), page 110.
4. Jerome Skilnick, *The Politics of Protest* (New York: Simon and Schuster, 1969), from Em Griffin, *Getting Together* (Downers Grove, Ill.: InterVarsity Press, 1982), page 135.

CHAPTER 9: HEART-TO-HEART COMBAT

1. Norman Shawchuck, *How to Manage Conflict in the Church* (Orland Park, Ill.: Spiritual Growth Resources,

1983), pages 13-19. If you want a copy of this excellent booklet, write the publisher at P.O. Box 1208, Orland Park, Illinois 60462. Phone: (312) 403-3151.

2. Shawchuck, page 26.
3. Romans 14:20, 1 Corinthians 8.
4. Shawchuck, page 27.
5. Philippians 2:3; Romans 12:16, 14:1.
6. Colossians 3:12, Romans 14:19, Galatians 5:22-23.
7. Romans 12:2, 1 Corinthians 6:9-10, James 2:17.
8. David Augsburger, *Caring Enough to Confront* (Ventura, Calif.: Regal Books, 1981), page 10.

CHAPTER 10: "LORD, TEACH US TO FIGHT"

1. Richard Stuart, *Helping Couples Change: A Social Learning Approach to Marital Therapy* (New York: The Guilford Press, 1980), page 292.

CHAPTER 11: THE CHURCH IN THE RING

1. C.R. Bach and P. Wyden, *The Intimate Enemy* (New York: William Marrow, 1969).
2. Original poem by one of the authors who is too ashamed to sign it! We will leave it to the reader to guess which of us is the bad poet.

Subject Index

Scripture Index

Living in Harmony Ministries

In 1980, James Hinkle and Tim Woodroof founded Living in Harmony Ministries, an effort dedicated to helping Christians fulfill Christ's command to love one another. *Among Friends* is an outgrowth of this ministry. Living in Harmony Ministries can be contacted at 2020 North 62nd Street, Lincoln, NE 68505.

SEMINARS

Seminars provide churches with a range of training to meet their particular needs: Among Friends (a basic primer on church relationships); The Urge to Merge (on developing intimacy); and Heart to Heart Conflict (on conflict management). Churches in over fifteen states have invited Hinkle and Woodroof to present one of their seminars.

VIDEO SERIES

An instructional thirteen-part video series provides congregations with an inexpensive means of exploring Christian relationships. Three tapes, containing over five hours of instruction, come with a planner's guide and study guide.

Over 300 congregations are presently making use of this tool.

CONSULTATION

The latest addition to this ministry consists of consulting services designed to provide congregations with practical help in three areas: Leadership Development, Congregational Relationship Analysis, and Conflict Mediation.